MY GRANNY USED TO SAY

To Sis. Nellie Stroud
God bless you!
Alana Watkins

MY GRANNY USED TO SAY

A 60-DAY DEVOTIONAL

ALANA WATKINS

TATE PUBLISHING
AND ENTERPRISES, LLC

My Granny Used to Say
Copyright © 2014 by Alana Watkins. All rights reserved.

No part of this publication may be reproduced, stored in a retrieval system or transmitted in any way by any means, electronic, mechanical, photocopy, recording or otherwise without the prior permission of the author except as provided by USA copyright law.

The opinions expressed by the author are not necessarily those of Tate Publishing, LLC.

Published by Tate Publishing & Enterprises, LLC
127 E. Trade Center Terrace | Mustang, Oklahoma 73064 USA
1.888.361.9473 | www.tatepublishing.com

Tate Publishing is committed to excellence in the publishing industry. The company reflects the philosophy established by the founders, based on Psalm 68:11,
"The Lord gave the word and great was the company of those who published it."

Book design copyright © 2014 by Tate Publishing, LLC. All rights reserved.
Cover design by Allen Jomoc
Interior design by Caypeeline Casas

Published in the United States of America

ISBN: 978-1-62994-432-6
Religion / Christian Life / Inspirational
13.12.16

DEDICATION

*In loving memory of my grandmother
Rosie Lee Scott Stone
(February 27, 1926–February 26, 2004)
She called me her sunshine; I called her my moon.*

ACKNOWLEDGMENTS

This is for you, Sweet Jesus. Freely I've received; now freely I give. May this work glorify you.

To Pastor Gregory Watkins, Sr., my loving and devoted husband, my spiritual guide, my best friend. No one has ever believed in me the way you do. I am *in love* with you, and "I thank my God upon every remembrance of you" (Philippians 1:3 kjv). Because of us, I am better. It's Jesus + you + me—*all the way*.

To my children Greg, Jr., and India, you give me oxygen and inspire me to breathe. I am abundantly blessed to call you my son and daughter. I love you so much, my gifts. To Sierra, I adore you to pieces. You add extra sweetness to my life, and I'm glad you're a part of it.

To my church family at Faith Tabernacle Apostolic Ministries. You keep me encouraged and uplifted in prayer, and I love you so much. We are one body, just as it should be, and I know in my heart that God is pleased with you. You represent the kingdom well.

To Karen Stone-Fry. My heart adores you to infinity and beyond. I can't remember a time in my life when it didn't melt at the thought of you. When God was passing out sisters, he gave me his absolute best. You are so dear to me, more dear than you'll ever know. May your cup run over.

To Prophetess Karen Watkins. You have been the wind beneath my wings throughout this process, and I thank God for you. Your prayers, your tears of joy and celebration with me (on my doorstep, in the church, in parking lots, or in the grocery store), along with your words of life spoken into me, have blessed me abundantly. Look what the Lord has done! (Deacon Mike, MJ, Marcus, and Amaya, I love you guys, too.)

To the Tate Publishing family. Thank you for giving life to my dream and a tablet to my vision. God told me to write it, and you gave me a place in the world to do just that. It was no coincidence.

CONTENTS

Introduction..15

Day 1:	The Pot Can't Call the Kettle Black.......	19
Day 2:	The Early Bird Catches the Worm	23
Day 3:	Nothing Comes to Sleepers but a Dream	27
Day 4:	A Watched Pot Never Boils...................	31
Day 5:	What's Done in the Dark Will Come to the Light................................	35
Day 6:	When God Made You He Broke the Mold	39
Day 7:	The Apple Doesn't Fall Far from the Tree	43
Day 8:	Every Time You Throw Dirt, You Lose a Little Ground.....................	47
Day 9:	A Penny Saved Is a Penny Earned.........	51
Day 10:	Don't Let Your Left Hand Know What Your Right Hand Is Doing..........	55

Day 11:	Anything Worth Having Is Worth Fighting For 59
Day 12:	A Hard Head Makes a Soft Behind 63
Day 13:	If You Make Your Bed Hard, You'll Have to Lie in It 67
Day 14:	All That Glitters Isn't Gold 71
Day 15:	An Empty Wagon Makes a Lot of Noise 77
Day 16:	A Stitch in Time Saves Nine 81
Day 17:	Beauty Is Only Skin Deep 85
Day 18:	Beauty Is in the Eyes of the Beholder 89
Day 19:	Don't Burn Your Bridges After You Cross Them 93
Day 20:	Blind in One Eye and Can't See out of the Other 97
Day 21:	It's Six in One Hand and Half a Dozen in the Other 101
Day 22:	Blood Is Thicker Than Water 105
Day 23:	Can't See the Forest for the Trees 109
Day 24:	Caught Between a Rock and a Hard Place 113
Day 25:	Clothes Don't Make the Man 117
Day 26:	Experience Is the Best Teacher 123
Day 27:	God Helps Those Who Help Themselves 127

Day 28:	God Moves in Mysterious Ways	131
Day 29:	You're Jumping Out of the Frying Pan and Into the Fire	135
Day 30:	Don't Count Your Chickens Before They Hatch	139
Day 31:	Birds of a Feather Flock Together	143
Day 32:	If You Lie with Dogs, You'll Get Up with Fleas	147
Day 33:	People in Glasshouses Shouldn't Throw Stones	151
Day 34:	Don't Bite the Hand That Feeds You	155
Day 35:	The Grass Is Always Greener on the Other Side of the Fence	159
Day 36:	Never Look a Gift Horse in the Mouth	163
Day 37:	Every Duck Praises His Own Pond	167
Day 38:	Everything That's Good to You Isn't Good for You	171
Day 39:	Beware of Wolves in Sheep's Clothing	175
Day 40:	Fools Rush in Where [Wise Men] Fear to Tread	179
Day 41:	To Err Is Human, to Forgive Divine	183

Day 42:	You Can't Pull the Wool over My Eyes	187
Day 43:	Fool Me Once, Shame on You; Fool Me Twice, Shame on Me	191
Day 44:	God Gave Me Two Ears and Only One Mouth So I Can Listen Twice as Much as I Speak	195
Day 45:	Everything That Comes Up Doesn't Have to Come Out	199
Day 46:	Don't Cut Off Your Nose to Spite Your Face	203
Day 47:	God Doesn't Like Ugly, and He's Not Stuck on Pretty!	207
Day 48:	Tell One Lie and You'll Have to Tell Two	211
Day 49:	A Whistling Woman and a Cackling Hen Always Come to No Good End	215
Day 50:	Think Before You Speak	219
Day 51:	Slow and Steady Wins the Race	223
Day 52:	The Hand That Rocks the Cradle Rules the World	227
Day 53:	An Idle Mind Is the Devil's Workshop	231
Day 54:	The Lord Will Put No More on You Than You Can Bear	235

Day 55:	Nothing Beats a Failure but a Try	241
Day 56:	United We Stand; Divided We Fall	245
Day 57:	Why Put Off for Tomorrow What You Can Do Today?	249
Day 58:	When Life Hands You Lemons Make Lemonade	253
Day 59:	Easy Come; Easy Go!	257
Day 60:	What Doesn't Kill You Makes You Stronger	261

INTRODUCTION

I am excited to share with you *My Granny Used to Say*, a daily devotional inspired by quotes and sayings that have been around for years, things we've all heard our grandparents or great grandparents say to guide us in everyday living.

Let me first tell you a little about the book's inspiration, Mrs. Rosie Lee Stone. She was my beloved and precious grandmother who passed away at the age of seventy-eight in 2004. Her heart held everyone she ever met, and she loved more than anyone I've ever known. When I was a small child, my family (my single-parent mother, my sister, and two brothers) and I lived across the street from my grandmother, whom we affectionately called *Ma Dear*. She was a constant in our lives and was dedicated to helping my mother rear us—leading, guiding, and teaching us along the way. She easily became my life's greatest influence. Over the years, I heard her say many expressions that she picked up "from the old folks." Many of these sayings served as offerings of encouragement, instruction, rebuke, and love. Many of them were funny, and even now, I smile when I hear them. Some she quoted from literature and was probably unaware she was actually quoting Alexander Pope. Some were just old sayings that had been around for ages.

What prompted me to write this book is the realization that many of these expressions have been lost. As a high school English teacher for fourteen years, I find that although some of these sayings remain among us, many have gone unspoken from generation to generation. I find myself having to translate "Don't cut off your nose to spite your face" or "Don't look a gift horse in the mouth." *My Granny Used to Say* brings many of these long-ago-forgotten expressions back for this generation to enjoy in the form of a devotional. Some of the timeless idioms that you'll see in the book are:

> The pot can't call the kettle black!
> God helps those who help themselves.
> Birds of a feather flock together.
> If you lie with dogs, you'll get up with fleas.
> Don't count your chickens before they hatch.
> People who live in glass houses shouldn't throw stones.
> Every duck praises his own pond.

In essence, I've taken all of the expressions I remember from the mouth of my grandmother (and other elderly people), given credit to the original sources when necessary, and matched each of them to a scripture that connects to the expression. The devotional study for each saying consists of either a story or commentary that illustrates the expression (or the related scripture). There is a lesson to be embraced in each page, and the result is a quaint, easy-to-read, yet spiritually rich devotional.

There are sixty sayings linked to Scripture and presented from a Christian perspective. *My Granny Used to Say* has that wonderful feel of yesteryear, and it is my prayer that it will warm the hearts of many around the country.

DAY 1:
THE POT CAN'T CALL THE KETTLE BLACK

> Let us not therefore judge one another any more.
>
> Romans 14:13 ASV

Back in the early '90s, The Williams Brothers released a gospel song titled "Sweep Around." The message of the song was clear—that everyone must clean his own house or take care of his own issues before shining a spotlight on the dirt that is in someone else's home. The chorus of the song says, "Sweep around your own front door before you try to sweep around mine," and as the song implies, nothing is more hypocritical than honing in on another person's flaws while being utterly flawed oneself. The Apostle Paul wrote in Philippians 3:12 NIV, "Not that I have already obtained all this, or have already been made perfect, but I press on to take hold of that for which Christ Jesus took hold of me." Living for Christ is a life of self-examination, and there is no time or place for judging others. I know that, for me personally, just keeping *myself* in order is a full time job!

When I was a little girl, there were moments in my life when I was both victim and perpetrator of viscous name calling, for children can be ruthless. Referring to one another as every animal on the farm, my siblings and I called each other everything from yellow cow or fat pig to Billy goat and skunk. One day, Ma Dear overheard us calling each other some rather interesting types of dogs; I mean a really bright array of dogs: ol' dog, black dog, stinky dog, and rabid dog, just to name a few. After listening to as much as she could take, Ma Dear called us in for a sit-down. I vividly remember her voice, shaken with anger and disappointment, asking us, "How can you call your brother or sister a dog when each of you came from the same woman? Your momma didn't give birth to *no* litter! And if she did, that would make all of you dogs. And what am I? Shame on you!" Ma Dear had a way of helping little eyes see big things, things from the perspective of family love and loyalty. There we stood as pots and kettles, calling one another black. Of course, we hadn't thought about the implications of our words quite as she presented them. In fact, we hadn't thought about our words *at all*. That particular day, we learned just how silly it is to insult one another when we share the same blood and so many ties that bind us.

Likewise, let us consider those with whom we share the redeeming blood of Jesus. Let us strive to be more compassionate and understanding toward our brothers and sisters, to lend a helping hand whenever we can, and to encourage and motivate them, not tear them down with our words or label them with our tongues.

The Word of God tells us, "if a man be overtaken in a fault, ye which are spiritual, restore such an one in the spirit of meekness; considering thyself, lest thou also be tempted" (Galatians 6:1 KJV). We should never add salt to the wounds of others through viscous criticism. Think about it. If I talk about Mary behind her back and slander her name as a liar, then who will condemn me as the gossiper I am? Who will label me as one who backbites or sows discord? There are no little sins or big sins in the lives of men and in God's eyes. "All unrighteousness is sin" (1 John 5:17 KJV), and sin is "an abomination unto the Lord" (Deuteronomy 25:16 KJV). Let's not be guilty of pointing fingers at the shortcomings of others when we ourselves stand on slippery slopes.

Time to think about it

What is God revealing to me through today's devotion?

_____

_____

_____

_____

What is one specific thing I can do to apply this lesson to my life?

_____

_____

_____

_____

DAY 2: THE EARLY BIRD CATCHES THE WORM

> Love not sleep, lest thou come to poverty; open thine eyes, and thou shalt be satisfied with bread.
>
> Proverbs 20:13 KJV

There's no feeling quite like that of rising early in the morning, before the day becomes cluttered with errands, chores, tasks, and responsibilities. Growing up in my grandmother's house taught me the beauty and benefit of rising early in the morning. Ma Dear wasn't one to tolerate laziness or slothfulness. Every morning, she would rise before daylight sat on the side of the horizon. She would make her way to the kitchen to prepare breakfast for us—and it wasn't cold cereal in those cute and handy little cardboard bowls either. We ate breakfasts reminiscent of Ma Dear's farming days and upbringing. Some mornings, the aroma of buttery grits, scrambled eggs, and smoked ham would rouse us from slumber. I loved when she cooked my favorite: her made-from-scratch pancakes with just a touch of lemon extract in the batter and oven-fried bacon pieces. If the smell of Ma Dear's mastery in the kitchen didn't bring us out hooked by our noses and floating half asleep, the shrill of her call would. "Renee! Karen! Ronnie! Sharron! Get up! It's time to get busy." And after breakfast, *busy* is exactly what we got. Ma Dear could assign chores like the most skilled and expert taskmaster. She knew what was to be accomplished and who was best for the job. If a chore required slow, meticulous work, then Karen was the girl for the job. If the task required speed and accuracy, then I was given that responsibility. As a result, Karen dusted, wiping the cracks and crevices of every little whatnot and returning them to their exact places on the coffee table, book shelf, end table, and window sill. I ran the dust mop, cleaned baseboards and windows, and washed dishes from the china cabinet. Along with our brothers, Ma Dear had Karen and me dusting, sweeping, polishing silver and hardwood floors, cleaning the bathroom until it reeked with Pine Sol, washing bedclothes, and beating throw rugs. When we worked together, we were usually done by noon and left with the rest of the day to enjoy the trivial aspects of youth. It would be an all-day event if we had vegetables to prepare for the freezer or fruit to chunk for preserves. Always, it was a time of togetherness, a time to laugh and talk, and a time to work and receive for our efforts. The feel and smell of a clean house was our reward; the fellowship of family was our pay; and the pride of a job well done was our bread. Having memories of those days and the time spent as a family accomplishing its goal has provided royalties that we still benefit from today.

My grandmother always said, "Hard work never hurt anyone," and she lived it by example. She was a virtuous woman who taught us the value of rising early to get the day done. Therefore, getting out of bed early in the morning became synonymous with diligence and dedication. In fact, rising early is universally associated with success. Best of all, it is a characteristic desired by those who seek to please God because rising early is a quality that God delights in seeing in his servants. The psalmist David wrote, "O GOD, thou art my God; early will I seek thee; my soul thirsteth for thee, my flesh longeth for thee in a dry and thirsty land, where no water is; To see thy power and thy glory, so as I have seen thee in the sanctuary. Because thy lovingkindness is better than life, my lips shall praise thee" (Psalm 63:1–3 KJV). When we hunger and thirst for God, he *will* satisfy us. When we seek him early, we *will* find him because in the wee hours of the morning, when the world is quietly at rest, God is wide awake and near.

Time to think about it

What is God revealing to me through today's devotion?

_____

_____

_____

_____

What is one specific thing I can do to apply this lesson to my life?

_____

_____

_____

_____

DAY 3:
NOTHING COMES TO SLEEPERS BUT A DREAM

> Wherefore he saith, Awake thou that sleepest, and arise from the dead, and Christ shall give thee light.
>
> Ephesians 5:14 KJV

We have all had that dream—the one from which we awake frightened, panicked, drenched in sweat, and relieved that it was only a dream. Also, we have all had that dream we didn't want to see end, the one that made us wish we could fall asleep again just to finish it. Whichever the case may be, whether relishing in a sweet dream or frantically escaping a nightmare, the succession of images, thoughts, or emotions that pass through the mind during sleep are arguably *unreal*. When we are asleep, life can only unfold before us in the form of dreams—those intangible imitations of life and illusions of living.

As Christians, we must arise from sleep. We must view it only as a necessary period of rest and a bridge between our days. Our days are precious gifts from God, and they are to be lived. We are not designed to reside in or be overly indulged in that resting state. We go there because we must, stay for a few hours as the body requires, but as soon as possible, we must be up and out, being about our father's business. Oscar Wilde said, "A dreamer is one who can only find his way by moonlight, and his punishment is that he sees the dawn before the rest of the world." That sounds pretty to the ears, but the reality is that unless the dreamer awakes from his sleep, he doesn't see the dawn at all. He who loves sleep can only dream, but it is he who rises to *live* who receives the reward of life.

Interestingly, as we lie down to sleep, our bodies rest in a supine position and mirrors the body's shape when it succumbs to death. The act of sleeping mimics the end of life, paralysis, and immobility. Life, however, in its glory, requires participation. Life in the daylight is awake and fruitful; it is productive and lived out to its fullest. Therefore, "awake thou that sleepest, and arise from the dead, and Christ shall give thee light" (Ephesians 5:14 KJV). Don't settle for mere images of life that pass through the mind during sleep. Don't even settle for the figments of your imaginations and imposters of your day dreams. Instead, enjoy your reality while being wide awake. Don't just dream, but *live*.

Time to think about it

What is God revealing to me through today's devotion?

_____

_____

_____

_____

What is one specific thing I can do to apply this lesson to my life?

_____

_____

_____

_____

DAY 4: A WATCHED POT NEVER BOILS

> Be careful for nothing; but in every thing by prayer and supplication with thanksgiving let your requests be made known unto God.
>
> Philippians 4:6 KJV

Of course, if one watches a pot of water heating on the stove long enough, it does eventually boil, but it takes a certain amount of patience and focus from the observer to reach that point. The anticipation and anxiety associated with waiting makes the climb to 212° F an eternity. Likewise, that is precisely what worrying does! It amplifies the discomfort of waiting. Isn't it a much better experience to hope in the Lord, to put our trust in him, and to wait on his grace and mercy? Isn't it a better choice to be about his business while we wait, not counting the hours but counting our blessings? God knows our every need, and he knows our heart's desires. Therefore, his word encourages us not to worry about anything, but to "delight [ourselves] also in the Lord and He shall give us the desires of [our] heart" (Psalm 37:4 KJV). Watching the pot doesn't make the water boil any faster. Watching the mailbox for that check doesn't make it come any sooner. Such acts only increase our level of stress, but when we commit our ways unto the Lord and trust in him, he will bring our blessings to pass (See Psalm 37:5 KJV).

God doesn't want us worrying about things. He wants his children to come to him in prayer and supplication with thanksgiving, making their requests known to him, and he will then provide perfect peace in the waiting season. When the time is right, we will receive for our faith and faithfulness the peace of God, which passes all understanding! It will keep our hearts and minds in Christ Jesus (See Philippians 4:6-7 KJV). Besides, Jesus asked in Matthew 6:27, "Which of you by taking thought can add one cubit unto his stature?" (KJV) He also said, "Take therefore no thought for the morrow: for the morrow shall take thought for the things of itself" (Matthew 6:34 KJV). Stay in the privilege and moment of resting in God and trusting in his sovereignty.

Often when I was a little girl, I stood in Ma Dear's kitchen with a pot of water on the stove, and I watched it to see if the water would strike a boil under my fixed and faithful eye. The result was always the same—a lack of focus or slipping of patience on my part. I typically became distracted by something else and moved on before the first bubble rose. By the time I returned to the pot of water, it was already boiling. Likewise, in life, if we get busy working for God, seeking his will for our lives and walking in his perfect way, the prayer or concern we've placed on the altar will be boiling over with blessings when we return to the pot. With our eyes focused on Jesus, he will always slip in and handle our cares, calm our fears, and increase our joy.

Time to think about it

What is God revealing to me through today's devotion?

_____

_____

_____

_____

What is one specific thing I can do to apply this lesson to my life?

_____

_____

_____

_____

DAY 5: WHAT'S DONE IN THE DARK WILL COME TO THE LIGHT

> For there is nothing covered, that shall not be revealed; neither hid, that shall not be known.
>
> Luke 12:2 KJV

Nothing we do is hidden from our God. He is omniscient and omnipresent, and nothing gets by him. Nothing escapes his infinite wisdom. As a mother, I have come to believe that God shares a bit of his wisdom in the hearts of parents, and we call it intuition. Sometimes we can *feel* when something isn't right with our children. We don't know exactly what it is, but we just *know* when they are going through something, and God leads us to pray. Other times, the Lord is more direct and simply exposes their misdeed.

The night before my son left home for college, he was driving to Sugarland, Texas, to meet a friend for dinner. On his way to the restaurant, he was stopped by a police officer for speeding and was cited for the violation, which was another issue altogether. Instead of telling his father and me about the incident, our son decided that he would handle it himself and just pay the ticket. I imagine he thought to himself, "My parents don't have to know. I'm a man now. I can take care of this myself. Besides, who wants to hear them fuss for an hour over a ticket?" Whatever he said to himself, it was enough to convince him to keep the incident a secret.

A couple of months later, a letter arrived from the Harris County Justice Court with a returned money order enclosed. According to the note attached, which was addressed to my son, the enclosed payment for the ticket could not be processed because the money order was not filled out. I read the letter several times before I eventually caved in laughter. My little darling had purchased a money order for over two hundred dollars and just dropped it in an envelope and mailed it in as payment for his ticket. After laughing for perhaps ten minutes, I settled into a gentle reminder of just how good God is to us, and I became very thankful. I was, first of all, thankful that he allowed an honest person to open the envelope. Second, despite my son's effort to pull the wool over his father's eyes and mine, I was somewhat proud of him for trying to handle this situation independently. He was, in a way, accepting responsibility for his actions and seeking to solve the problem on his own. As I think about him and his past antics, I realize that he has grown into an amazing young man, and he has learned a lot about being responsible and making wise decisions. However, one lesson seemed to have been repeated throughout his life and that is: What is done in the darkness *will* come to light. He has always been one who could never get away with anything, and I believe it has made him to be the honest and open man that he is today.

As children of the Most High, we cannot get away with anything either, especially before the all-seeing eyes of God. We may as well walk upright before him because, as children of light, darkness just doesn't suit us.

Time to think about it

What is God revealing to me through today's devotion?

_____

_____

_____

_____

What is one specific thing I can do to apply this lesson to my life?

_____

_____

_____

_____

DAY 6: WHEN GOD MADE YOU HE BROKE THE MOLD

> There is neither Jew nor Greek, there is neither bond nor free, there is neither male nor female: for ye are all one in Christ Jesus.
>
> Galatians 3:28 KJV

We are all God's creation and are loved unconditionally, regardless of age, sex, race, or nationality. We are specially designed by God, and he is no respecter of persons, but he loves us all *uniquely* the same. The Holy Bible says in Genesis 1, "In the beginning God created the heaven and the earth" (v. 1 KJV). "God also said let there be light: and there was light" (v. 3 KJV). Later in verse 11, God said, "Let the earth bring forth grass, the herb yielding seed, and the fruit tree yielding fruit after his kind" (KJV). He said, "Let the waters bring forth abundantly the moving creature that hath life, and fowl that may fly above the earth" (v. 20 KJV). God then called for the earth [to] bring forth the living creature after his kind, cattle, and creeping thing, and beast of the earth after his kind: and it was so (v. 24 KJV). These were all in obedience to his word.

Finally, on the sixth day of creation, God formed and made humankind. Genesis 1:27 says, "So God created man in his own image, in the image of God created he him; male and female created he them" (KJV). Close examination of the creation reveals that initially, God only *spoke*, and the elements of creation *obeyed* him. The beauty that we see in our natural world every day—the blue sky, the white clouds, the evening sky that is sometimes veiled with streaks of pink or gray or peach or silver—all moved, stopped, formed, and reformed at the voice of God. Even the snail and the caterpillar heeded the imagination of the Father. But unlike all of these other creations, man was *handmade*, picked up and molded from the dust of the ground—personally made. Then God breathed into man's nostrils, and he became a living soul. Since the creation of the first man Adam, God has not ceased to make and mold mankind in his image, yet we are all special and unique.

God is still making and perfecting his creation. He is working in each of us, shaping us continually. Ecclesiastes 3:11 says, "He hath made everything beautiful in his time" (KJV). That means that you; yes, *you* are beautiful, and he delights in you. Verse 14 of the same passage says, "I know that whatsoever God doeth, it shall be forever; nothing can be put to it, nor anything taken from it" (KJV). This word assures us that what we make of ourselves may be temporary, but what God makes of us is eternal.

Think about our eternal design and uniqueness. No two human beings are exactly the same. Our God is an intricate and masterful painter who has created skin hues of ivory and pink; beige and brown; bronze and ebony black. He has numbered the hairs on our heads and given some people coils and coarseness, some bouncing curls, and some silky straightness. He has designed the prints of each of our fingertips to be unique, and then he broke the mold. While I think on these things, it comforts my heart because it speaks of God's exclusive love for us. He doesn't become tired of us wrestling against his hands, and he doesn't toss us on the shelf, saying, "Oh, I can't do anything with this thing! I'm done." No, God continues to form this clay. Personally, I hear him say to me as he did to the house of Israel in Jeremiah 18:6, "O, [*Alana,*] cannot I do with you as this potter? Behold as the clay is in the potter's hand, so are ye in mine hand" (KJV). We are all clay in his hands, a painting on his canvas, pure ivory or precious bronze carefully sculpted by God. He is a wonderful Creator, and we are blessed to be one of his original pieces.

Yes, we are priceless works of art, and the Lord God Almighty is the artist. Knowing this, we can say as David said, "I will praise thee; for I am fearfully and wonderfully made" (Psalm 139:14 KJV). Our hope rests in God's promise that "He who began a good work in [us] will carry it to completion" (Philippians 1:6 KJV), making us perfect *in* Him.

Time to think about it

What is God revealing to me through today's devotion?

_____
_____
_____
_____

What is one specific thing I can do to apply this lesson to my life?

_____
_____
_____
_____

DAY 7: THE APPLE DOESN'T FALL FAR FROM THE TREE

> Even so every good tree bringeth forth good fruit; but a corrupt tree bringeth forth evil fruit.
>
> Matthew 7:17 KJV

As a child growing up in Natchez, Mississippi, I spent many summer days playing with friends in their backyards, or even the backyards of our childless neighbors and mother figures. Most of the women who lived in my neighborhood were homemakers and masters of canning and preserving fruit, so naturally, they grew a fruit-bearing tree of some kind in their yards. Miss Marguerite had a peach tree. Miss Love had plum trees, a huge pear tree, and a gorgeous Magnolia I have to mention. Sweet Mama had plum trees—the best in the neighborhood, and a fig tree. The Ivorys had plum trees next to the outhouse. Miss Estelle and Miss Alberta had pear trees, three in a row. My Ma Dear had a peach tree that only produced green, little knots longing to be peaches, and my mama had a fig tree and what I believe was a boysenberry in the corner of her small yard. It was typical to stop during the day and pick fruits of all kinds from wherever we roamed. Dewberries grew along the fences of some yards and were scattered in nearby vacant lots that were once gardens. When my siblings and I visited my great grandmother, Mama Queen, in Ferriday, Louisiana, we were still exposed to the joy of being near the sweet ripeness of many fruits. Mama Queen lived near a crawfish pond, and on the side of the pond, opposite her house, grew muscadines, which bootleggers used to make wine, and golden, plump persimmons that left your taste buds dancing. So as a child, I noticed and enjoyed everything about fruit—from the exhilaration of every sweet bite to the feel of squashed fruit beneath my bare feet and overripe pulp between my toes.

Like fruit trees remembered from my childhood, children of God are known by the fruit they bear. Fruit that is uncharacteristic of a pear tree, for example, is not found on its branches. Neither is such fruit naturally found on the ground beneath the pear tree because, whatever the fruit may be, it does not fall far from the tree that bore it. Likewise, when we are engrafted into the family of God, our attributes must reflect the God of heaven in whom we reside and who resides in us. Jesus said that we are the branches, and he is the true vine (See John 15:1, 5 KJV). The Word of God also instructs the children of God to be fruitful. Knowing this, we must "bring forth *good* fruit" (See Matthew 7:17 KJV and Luke 6:43 KJV) for nothing of Jesus is corrupt. When we are harvested in Christ Jesus and

Christ Jesus harvested in us, the fruit we produce—and by-product of our lives—will bear stark resemblance to the Master's. He is the prototype of what his children should be. And what is *of him* is certainly not far *from him*.

Time to think about it

What is God revealing to me through today's devotion?

_____

_____

_____

_____

What is one specific thing I can do to apply this lesson to my life?

_____

_____

_____

_____

DAY 8:
EVERY TIME YOU THROW DIRT, YOU LOSE A LITTLE GROUND

> Be not deceived; God is not mocked: for whatsoever a man soweth, that shall he also reap.
>
> Galatians 6:7 KJV

What are you storing up? Are you reaping the blessings of God because you are a constant source of blessings to others, or are you chased and pursued by misfortunes because of your apathy toward others? How we choose to treat other people is a true indication of how we may expect to be treated by others. It is the law of sowing and reaping, and this law never fails. When we treat others will love and respect, we sow in the spiritual soil of love and respect. If we are generous, the fruit we produce is generosity. Likewise, if we sow bitterness and discord, those are the weeds we will surely see in harvest.

Being mean to others is easy, especially when they have offended or hurt us. The easy choice and instinct of many is to lash out and seek revenge. However, it takes a disciplined and spirit-led person to turn the other cheek. Jesus said, "If someone strikes you on one cheek, turn to him the other also. If someone takes your cloak, do not stop him from taking your tunic" (Luke 6:29 NIV). When we lash out at people, we may feel momentary satisfaction in the flesh, but we lose ground in the spirit.

Jesus has called us to be witnesses of him—of his grace and his mercy—and it isn't always easy. The high road is also the hard road sometimes, but we must ask ourselves a question (or two). How can I live a life that speaks of his mercy *toward me* and *in me* if I am merciless? How can I speak to others of his forgiveness *of me* and *in me* if I forgive not? I have had to forgive people for hurting me, violating me in the worst way. Was it fun? No. Did I like it? No. Did I even want to do it? Not likely. However, the tragic alternative to forgiveness is to create a haven for unforgiveness—to harbor anger and wrath inside our hearts. Such emotions are detrimental. They throw dirt, and when they do, the soul of the thrower loses ground. His or her soul loses peace. His or her soul loses joy. His or her soul loses the forgiveness and hope that Jesus offers him. Given the choice, let's choose to sow forgiveness, for "anger [rests] in the bosom of fools" (Ecclesiastes 7:9 KJV). Forgiving those who have harmed us is not an easy task. It is, however, paramount to experiencing the peace and forgiveness of God. Jesus said, "For if ye forgive men their trespasses, your heavenly Father will also forgive you" (Matthew 6:14 KJV). In the kingdom of our Lord, none who have received God's forgiveness can afford to lose ground. Let us, therefore, drop the dirt and cleanse our hands for with this, the Lord is pleased.

Time to think about it

What is God revealing to me through today's devotion?

_____

_____

_____

_____

What is one specific thing I can do to apply this lesson to my life?

_____

_____

_____

_____

DAY 9: A PENNY SAVED IS A PENNY EARNED

> Go to the ant, thou sluggard; consider her ways, and be wise: which having no guide, overseer, or ruler, provideth her meat in the summer, and gathereth her food in the harvest.
>
> Proverbs 6:6–8 KJV

I once heard a preacher say, "Where there is no hope in the future, there is no power in the present." How true! This statement is particularly powerful when applied to putting away and saving for a rainy day. Sadly, we are living in a right now, instantaneous, microwave-dependent society. We want *what* we want *when* we want it. This attitude has moved our thinking away from layaway plans to credit card debt. However, a wise and thoughtful steward knows the benefits of delayed gratification, wise investments, and putting away for tomorrow. An early English saying states that a fool and his money are soon parted, and the scriptures support it. The Word of God admonishes believers to look to the ways of the ant, who is wise, because she has no overseer or ruler standing over her to make her prepare for tomorrow. Still, she makes herself ready in the summer so that when the harsh and inevitable winter comes upon her, she will survive. (See Proverbs 6:6-8).

In the natural, many of us do strive to put money into retirement plans, 401(k)s, IRAs (Individual Retirement Account) and certificates of deposit, money market, and other interest-bearing accounts. Those who are prudent plan for the day when they will not have a steady income and will need a financial strategy to maintain their quality of life. The best of the prudent also learn to cut corners, to seek out the best deals for their money, using discounts, sales, and coupons to spend less and save more. Surely, such practices are wise, and when the day of need arrives, that penny saved is just as valuable and spendable as the one earned in work.

The same forethought and diligence must be applied in our spiritual walk. Jesus said in Matthew 6:19–21 KJV

> Lay not up for yourselves treasures upon earth, where moth and rust doth corrupt, and where thieves break through and steal: But lay up for yourselves treasures in heaven, where neither moth nor rust doth corrupt, and where thieves do not break through nor steal: For where your treasure is, there will your heart be also.

When the child of God stores away deeds of righteousness by living a life set aside and dedicated to glorifying God, he is making a deposit into an eternal fund. However, he is not saved by works for salvation comes by the grace of God, and it is only because of

God's mercies that God's stewards are not consumed. Nevertheless, righteous deposits of faith in Jesus, salvation in his name, and being sold out to him gives us the privilege to expect that he will hear us when we call, catch us when we fall, and be with us to the very end. And that is an awesome and eternal return on such a small investment!

Time to think about it

What is God revealing to me through today's devotion?

_____

_____

_____

_____

What is one specific thing I can do to apply this lesson to my life?

_____

_____

_____

_____

DAY 10: DON'T LET YOUR LEFT HAND KNOW WHAT YOUR RIGHT HAND IS DOING

> But when you give to the needy, do not let your left hand know what your right hand is doing.
>
> Matthew 6:3 NIV

Performing random acts of kindness, paying it forward, leaving anonymous gifts—such measures should be done regularly by all who love the Lord. We are the hands of Jesus, and he touches the lives of the needy with *his hands*. However, do not look for the praises of men when performing the goodness of God. Show love as if on a secret mission from the Father—to bless someone and go unnoticed, to bless someone and let all the glory go to God.

It's a sad truth that sometimes, people perform good deeds, not out of the goodness of their hearts but out of their pride and need for praise. Jesus said, "So when you give to the needy, do not announce it with trumpets, as the hypocrites do in the synagogues and on the streets, to be honored by men. I tell you the truth, they have received their reward in full" (Matthew 6:2 NIV). The Word of God also says to "[do] nothing out of selfish ambition or vain conceit, but in humility consider others better than yourselves" (Philippians 2:3 NIV). When we perform an act of kindness, it should be done as unto the Lord, esteeming the poor as better than ourselves. Our alms must be done with humility and a sincere desire to bless those who are in need.

As followers of Christ, we are compelled to give and help the poor. Jesus instructed the rich young ruler to sell all that he had and give it to the poor that he might have eternal life (see Matthew 19:21). The early church fulfilled Jesus' instruction so that all men could have their needs supplied (see Acts 4:32–37). The Old Testament, likewise, bears witness that God made provision for the poor. "But the seventh year thou shalt let it rest and lie still; that the poor of thy people may eat" (Exodus 23:11 KJV). The body of Christ exists to show forth the love, kindness, and generosity of Jesus. However, the motive should not be the applause and praises of men. If so, the Bible tells us that we have our reward—the praises of men. But if we show love anonymously, humbly, and quietly, then God is pleased with us, and all the glory belongs to him.

We do these things as unto the Lord, not as unto men. Who do you want to please, God or man? If you seek to please man, you can't be a servant of Christ (see Galatians 1:10 KJV). Today, go out and show forth the love of the God who lives in you, and do it not that men may give you a name but do it because you are called by his name! Perform a random act of kindness without anyone knowing about it. God will see you and be pleased!

Time to think about it

What is God revealing to me through today's devotion?

_____

_____

_____

_____

What is one specific thing I can do to apply this lesson to my life?

_____

_____

_____

_____

DAY 11: ANYTHING WORTH HAVING IS WORTH FIGHTING FOR

> I have fought the good fight, I have finished the race, and I have remained faithful. And now the prize awaits me—the crown of righteousness, which the Lord, the righteous Judge, will give me on the day of his return. And the prize is not just for me but for all who eagerly look forward to his appearing.
>
> 2 Timothy 4:7-8 NLT

Several years ago, in my seventh grade language arts class, we were studying a poem written in the 1800s by Emma Lazarus. The title of the poem is "The New Colossus," and we know it so well today because the last few lines of the poem are engraved on the base of the Statue of Liberty:

> Keep ancient lands, your storied pomp!
> Cries she with silent lips.
> Give me your tired, your poor,
> Your huddled masses yearning to breathe free,
> The wretched refuse of your teeming shore.

> Send these, the homeless, tempest-tossed to me,
> I lift my lamp beside the golden door.

While teaching the poem, I became moved by the words, and in an effort to help my students fully appreciate the meaning of the verse, I showed them a video about immigration to America during the late 1800s and early 1900s. According to the video, from 1880–1920 over eight million immigrants came to this country from Europe, Africa, Asia, and various parts of the world—all in search of a better life. The video showed how these men, women, and children endured poor living conditions aboard steamships, sleeping on narrow bunks in the ship's steerage, going without showers, and being cramped in small, foul-smelling compartments. Once they arrived on Ellis Island, they endured hours of examinations—both physical and mental. The process was rigorous and extremely difficult, but in the minds of the immigrants, the hardship was worth it. America—the land of the free, which promised unlimited opportunities and a chance to start over—had become home, and these sojourners from faraway places fought diligently to get here. As they sailed into the harbor of Ellis Island, I imagine they felt as if their every dream was finally within reach, hope was at their fingertips, and peace and protection were in the palms of their hands. The dream was worth fulfilling, so their struggles were worth enduring.

As I began to tell my students about Emma Lazarus's poem, I could see their little faces grow more and more attentive as the poem's words came to life for them. It was as if they could feel the spirit of welcome that came from the words. The Statue of Liberty stands with her right arm stretched high and a torch in her hand, lighting the way for those in search of something better. Those who roamed needed not to roam anymore. They could settle and enjoy the benefits of freedom and home. Today, the Statue of Liberty symbolizes America's opened arms and speaks to the native lands of those who have settled here. She begs of them, "Give me your tired," those who have roamed and are wearied from their journey. She says to them: "Give me your poor," those who are without and in need; "Give me your huddled masses, yearning to breathe free," those who are oppressed and afflicted but are seeking freedom and hope for a better life; "Give me your wretched refuse," those who are thrown away or discarded as rubbish; "Give to me your tempest-tossed," human souls battered by the storms of life, tossed to and fro and unsettled; "Give them all to me, send them my way. I lift my light beside this golden door."

As I taught this lesson, my mind fell on my Lord and Savior, Jesus Christ. I envisioned him on that rugged cross—not a sculpture of clay or copper but a flesh-and-blood man. There he hung with outstretched arms, calling unto man, and he cries still, "Come unto me, all ye that labor and are heavy laden, and I will give you rest. Take my yoke upon you, and learn of me; for I am meek and lowly in heart, and ye shall find rest unto your souls" (Matthew 11:28–29 KJV).

Long ago, those immigrants came to America with nothing but their faith in a piece of land and the spirit of democracy that governed it. Today, Jesus says, "I am the way, the truth and the life" (John 14:6 KJV). He stands at the door welcoming us, and if we enter that door with faith in him, our tomorrow is limitless.

Time to think about it

What is God revealing to me through today's devotion?

_____

_____

_____

_____

What is one specific thing I can do to apply this lesson to my life?

_____

_____

_____

_____

DAY 12: A HARD HEAD MAKES A SOFT BEHIND

> CHILDREN, obey your parents in the Lord: for this is right.
>
> Ephesians 6:1 KJV

A hard head makes a soft behind. In other words, there are consequences for disobedience, especially disobedience to parents. In my personal walk with God, I have learned to embrace the idea that God is my *Father*. In Galatians 4, the Bible tells believers that we are his adopted children and that God sent forth his only begotten son that we all might receive the adoption of sons (v. 4 KJV). Therefore, when we read scriptures like Philippians 1:6 KJV, "He who began a good work in you will carry it on to completion," we may see his work in us as he rears us. He's bringing us up much like we bring up our own children. Just as we desire a meaningful relationship with our own sons and daughters and take the time to teach them right from wrong to mold them into people with purpose, so does our Heavenly Father. He knows us through and through—our likes and dislikes, our tastes, our temperaments, our strengths, and weaknesses. Just as we know our children, he knows us. And in his excellence in parenting, God has given us his Spirit, his DNA, that he might lead us along life's path. Armed with the genes of his holiness and the road map of his Word, how can we get lost or go astray? By disobedience.

Everything that concerns us about our own children (the things we try to teach them), be they infant or aged, are the same things that concern God about us: what they eat/what we eat (naturally and spiritually), their happiness/our happiness, how they dress when they leave the house/how we dress when we leave the house, the way they treat other people/the way we treat others, their general welfare/our general welfare, the words they speak/the words we speak, the music, television programs, and books they read/our music, television shows, and books. We are no different in God's eyes. Just as we readily admit that our children must be taught—and we teach them—we must also recognize our need to learn and allow God, our Father, to take care of us. Let us rest in him, trust him, and obey him.

The old folks used to say, "A hard head makes a soft behind," and we certainly don't want to reap from a harvest of disobedience. When we are unwilling to do as our Father instructs, the result we experience may be developmental delay, stunted growth, or spiritual deformity. God is trying to complete a work in us; let us allow him to finish it. One day, we will reach maturity, having grown in grace and knowledge. Well-defined boundaries will create in us a well-defined Christian.

We will then be able to go out in the vocation for which God has prepared us, and he will be able to recommend us with joy.

Time to think about it

What is God revealing to me through today's devotion?

_____

_____

_____

_____

What is one specific thing I can do to apply this lesson to my life?

_____

_____

_____

_____

DAY 13:
IF YOU MAKE YOUR BED HARD, YOU'LL HAVE TO LIE IN IT

> But he that doeth wrong shall receive for the wrong which he hath done: and there is no respect of persons.
>
> Colossians 3:25

Accepting responsibility for one's actions is slowly becoming a dwindling virtue nowadays. On television, we see people seeking exoneration for crimes they have actually committed and forgiveness for deeds they have done without remorse and about which they even boast. More and more, we are becoming a people who want to dance to the piper's music and then stiff him on the bill. Still, the Word of God stands true. The Bible clearly reveals to us the law of sowing and reaping. It may be in this world or maybe in the world to come, "[but] he that doeth wrong shall receive for the wrong which he hath done; and there is no respect of person" (Colossians 3:25 KJV). We should all take heed to treat everyone we meet with the love of Christ that abides in our hearts. To do otherwise creates a hard bed and restless nights.

Galatians 6:7–9 KJV states, "Be not deceived; God is not mocked: for whatsoever a man soweth, that shall he also reap. For he that soweth to his flesh shall of the flesh reap corruption; but he that soweth to the Spirit shall of the Spirit reap life everlasting. And let us not be weary in well doing: for in due season we shall reap, if we faint not." Even in the beauty and magnificence of God's plan of redemption for mankind, he does not necessarily remove the earthly consequences for our sins. He takes away the stains of our iniquities and removes eternal damnation, but sometimes we must deal with the aftermath of the hurt and harm we have inflicted upon others. A prime example of this truth exists in the Book of Truths in the life of King David.

David allows lust for another man's wife to take root in his heart when, from his rooftop, he witnesses Uriah's wife, Bathsheba, washing her body. He allows his lust for her to lead him further into sin—into the grips of covetousness, adultery, lies and deception, and even murder. Although David repents before God when the prophet Nathan reveals David's state of wickedness to him, David still suffers consequences. Yes, God forgives David for Nathan says to him, "The LORD… hath put away thy sin; thou shalt not die" (2 Samuel 12:13 KJV). However, David's first son, who is conceived in sin with Bathsheba, dies. There is more: David's son Amnon rapes his half-sister Tamar, and in an act of vengeance, David's other son and Tamar's full brother, Absalom, kills Amnon. David endures pain, agony, and the dysfunction of his family as a harvest ripened by his own sin. To add insult to injury, Absalom also sleeps with David's concubines and leads a full rebellion against David, ultimately dying at the hands of David's servant Joab in the Battle of Mount Ephraim (see II Samuel chapters 11-14).

David's life serves as a cautionary tale to abide in righteousness that we may reap the blessings of God. Sow love and reap love. Sow peace and reap peace. Sow joy and reap joy unspeakable. Stay in God's will and reap his plan and purpose for your life. In other words, make your bed soft and reap the comforts of perfect rest.

Time to think about it

What is God revealing to me through today's devotion?

_____

_____

_____

_____

What is one specific thing I can do to apply this lesson to my life?

_____

_____

_____

_____

DAY 14: ALL THAT GLITTERS ISN'T GOLD

> But Abraham said, Son, remember that thou in thy lifetime receivedst thy good things, and likewise Lazarus evil things: but now he is comforted, and thou art tormented.
>
> Luke 16:25 KJV

Every year, believers and nonbelievers around the world celebrate Christmas. What a beautiful season! For one month, *mankind* basks in good will—singing carols and decorating their homes, neighborhoods, and city streets. Everyone is busy shopping for gifts, cooking sweets and treats, laughing aloud, and spreading good cheer in honor of the Savior's birth. Sometimes, I wonder about it all, asking myself if we are perhaps creating a counterfeit image of the true life of Christ. Does the festive presentation make his life and death on earth more palatable to us, easier to think about and accept? The problem is people have a tendency to transfer these glowing images into their expectation of what life in Christ is like, and they end up overlooking the beauty that is found in the modesty and humbleness, the servitude, and even the ugliness of Jesus's time on earth.

Isaiah 53:2 NIV says, "He grew up before him like a tender shoot, and like a root out of dry ground. He had no beauty or majesty to attract us to him, nothing in his appearance that we should desire him." Jesus never intended for us to beautify his passion with glimmer and glam. He doesn't take pleasure in such superficial presentation of him in an effort to entice the world—appealing to the lusts of their eyes. Doing this minimizes the agonizing passion of our Lord and Savior and his *true beauty* that is only spiritual in nature.

Jesus gave up the extravagant, the fancy, glorified image when he left heaven and came to earth. Yet we cling to that picture of him, even when we imagine him moving about in flesh. The Word of God says, "For we know the grace of our Lord Jesus Christ, that, though he was rich, yet for your sakes he became poor, that ye through his poverty might be rich" (2 Corinthians 8:9 KJV). Jesus himself declares, "Foxes have holes, and birds of the air have nests, but the Son of Man has no place to lay his head" (Matthew 8:20 NIV). He came not to appeal to the comfort and eyes of man but to man's willingness to humble himself and be like Christ.

Jesus Christ, the Son of the Living God, was born in a stable, wrapped in swaddling clothes, and laid in a manger. As pretty as the world attempts to make that scene in Bethlehem appear, with bright stars and glowing lights around his bed, in reality, Jesus was born like all babies—crying and covered in the blood and fluids of his mother's womb. He was wrapped tightly in whatever cloth his mother had available and then placed in the trough from which the animals fed. There was no light other than perhaps the dim moonlight and a candle or lantern to light the otherwise pitch-black shelter. Surrounding him were sounds and smells of beasts nearby. It was not a shining scene but a harsh reminder of just how much the Lord loves us and how much he chose to endure for our redemption.

Even his death on the cross is sensationalized by man so that we can look to it in awe and wonder. The crucifix has been molded in gold and shaped in silver. It has been painted in rich oils and vibrant watercolors. It has been hailed as a beautiful sight when in reality there is nothing pretty about it. It was a scene of pain and suffering, of one man nailed to a cross in anguish. We can't imagine the pain. Our minds shut out the spasms and convulsions he must have had as his body bled out and died. Our minds shut out the flies and insects drawn to the smell and spill of his blood. Our minds shut out the urine and excrements that might have escaped his body and coursed down his legs, and the blood thickening, coagulating at his wounds. Isaiah 53:3 NIV says, "He was despised and rejected by men, a man of sorrows, and familiar with suffering…" However, we've created pretty little golden images of him to esteem, while the true and living savior "took up our infirmities and carried our sorrows, yet we considered him stricken by God, smitten by him, and afflicted" (v. 4).

Let us be mindful of the authentic spiritual and inner beauty of Jesus Christ, not the outward images fashioned by men. The appeal of Jesus is not on the outside. It is on the inside. It is a spiritual attraction that draws us to his love, his joy, his peace, his longsuffering, his gentleness, his goodness, his faith, his meekness, and his temperance. It is a spiritual attraction that draws us to his pain and suffering and leads us to the question "What must I do to be saved?"

First Samuel 16:7 KJV reads, "But the LORD said unto Samuel, Look not on his countenance, or on the height of his stature; because I have refused him: for the LORD seeth not as man seeth; for man looketh on the outward appearance, but the LORD looketh on the hearts." Let us look on the heart of Jesus today so that we might experience him according to Philippians 3:10 (KJV), and that is to "know Christ and the power of his resurrection and the fellowship of sharing in his sufferings, becoming like him in his death." Nothing about Jesus appeals to this flesh! We are drawn by the spiritual beauty of grace. Let us not forget that as we think on him now and forever.

Time to think about it

What is God revealing to me through today's devotion?

_____

_____

_____

_____

What is one specific thing I can do to apply this lesson to my life?

_____

_____

_____

_____

DAY 15: AN EMPTY WAGON MAKES A LOT OF NOISE

> The tongue of the wise useth knowledge aright:
> but the mouth of fools poureth out foolishness.
>
> Proverbs 15:2

We all have seen it play out before our eyes—that moment when the one with the *least* to say speaks *loudest*. We have all seen the loser of a debate, the person who has the weakest points of an argument, grow angry, yell and speak louder than his opponent who makes complete and perfect sense. He is like the politician who, when he runs out of valid points to make in his debate, resorts to mudslinging, name-calling, and slander. In other words, the empty wagon starts to make a lot of noise.

It's funny how everyone wants to have the last word. Yet the Word of God tells us, "Even a fool, when he holds his peace, is counted wise" (Proverbs 17:28 KJV). To the world, however, he who does not speak up is weak. Those who defend themselves are lauded and esteemed. I'm reminded of the scripture in Isaiah 53, which reads, "He was oppressed, and he was afflicted, *yet he opened not his mouth*: he is brought as a lamb to the slaughter, and as a sheep before her shearers is dumb, *so he openeth not his mouth*" (v. 7 KJV [emphasis mine]). What a perfect example of humility and quietness. The Word of God instructs us to "study to be quiet" (I Thessalonians 4:11 KJV). That's how important it is.

Let us not be empty vessels spewing out useless noise, rattling about, revealing emptiness. Let us be wise with our lips, having spirits that are controlled by the Holy Ghost, disciplined in righteousness so that when we speak, our voices will be heard for the right reasons—because of the wisdom and knowledge coming forth and not because our volume is decibels above everyone else's. We want our words to be seasoned, timely, and meaningful.

Time to think about it

What is God revealing to me through today's devotion?

_____

_____

_____

_____

What is one specific thing I can do to apply this lesson to my life?

_____

_____

_____

_____

DAY 16:
A STITCH IN TIME SAVES NINE

> And whatsoever ye do, do it heartily, as to the Lord, and not unto men.
>
> Colossians 3:23 KJV

When threads in your jeans start to wear thin on the knees or when you have a slight rip in your pants that requires only a stitch or two, catching that rip when it first happens will save you a lot more time and effort than if you wait until later, at which point, nine stitches may be required. Ma Dear was a seamstress, and she had an eye for the wear and tear of clothing. At the first sign of a frayed garment, she took out her patches, a needle and thread, and a steam iron, and she went to work. Her doing so extended the life of the garment and saved her from having to do more work later. We, the children of God, can learn a lot about stitching in time. Think about it. Over time, a constant stream of water can erode even the greatest rock. So why put off a small rip for tomorrow when it can be mended today? Why not nip *whatever it is* in the bud *now*?

As a teacher and student, I have found that for most people, it is far better to study for exams along the way than attempting to learn it all in one night. Of course, cramming for tests does place the information in one's short-term memory, and this method will get him or her by for the moment, but when a student, over a grading period, consistently takes a little time to learn information, revisit it, and meditate on that information, he or she acquires lasting knowledge. As another saying goes, "An ounce of prevention is worth a pound of cure."

Learning to deal with situations in the moment and as they come is a valuable lesson that applies to so many areas of our lives. We must recognize that procrastination is the thief of time (Edward Young, 1683–1765), and it leads to unnecessary stress and anxiety. The Bible tells us to be careful for nothing (see Philippians 4:6 KJV), but to take everything to God! In other words, don't *worry* about a thing, but trust God! And taking care of business sooner, opposed to later, greatly reduces the burden of having to race against time. Let us strive to stay on top of things in our lives. Put out fires as they spark—not waiting until they become full-blown blazes or runaway wildfires before attempting to extinguish them. We risk irreparable damage when we let the blazes grow. We lose control of the task that has become too great to manage. So when you're tempted to put something off until later, especially something you can knock out in just a few minutes *now*, be proactive and do it. Stress the urgency of *now*, and get it done. You'll be glad you did.

Time to think about it

What is God revealing to me through today's devotion?

_____

_____

_____

_____

What is one specific thing I can do to apply this lesson to my life?

_____

_____

_____

_____

DAY 17: BEAUTY IS ONLY SKIN DEEP

> Favour is deceitful, and beauty is vain: but a woman that feareth the LORD, she shall be praised.
>
> Proverbs 31:30

Whenever I hear this expression, I hear the voices of the Temptations, singing their 1966 hit by the same title. The idea is that physical beauty runs second to inner beauty. I hear David Ruffin crooning, "Now friends ask what do I see in you, but it goes deeper than the eye can view." That is a perfect description of the kind of beauty mentioned in Psalm 149:4 (KJV). "For the LORD taketh pleasure in his people: he will beautify the meek with salvation." The beauty of God's people goes deeper than the eye can see, deeper than the mere surface beauty of pretty eyes, rosy cheeks, and luscious lips. The beauty of God's people radiates from within and glows like a soft fire in a dark and dank world.

I love to watch people. Sometimes when I'm in the mall or at a public event, I watch the people around me because I think we are such fascinating creatures. Occasionally, I see couples who strike me as mismatched. For whatever reason, they don't *look* as if they would be attracted to one another. Maybe one seems gregarious and extrovert while the other seems quiet or shy. Through these couples, even my own life, I've realized that true love is not about what is on the outside. It's natural to be physically attracted to a person, but deep and meaningful, lasting love has to be based on something more. If it isn't, what happens when the beauty fades? If love is based only on what the eyes of the beholder calls beauty, then it would be as thin and shallow as the depth of a person's skin, and that's pretty thin.

The Lord loves us unconditionally with a love that has nothing to do with how physically attractive we are, and likewise, we must not be fooled by the outer appearance of others. To simply put it, don't judge a book by its cover. I'm now reminded of the cross of Calvary and the unattractiveness it portrays on the surface. Its sheer and utter beauty lies beneath. Isaiah 53:2 (NIV) says, "He had no beauty or majesty to attract us to him, nothing in his appearance that we should desire him." Yet, Jesus draws men to the cross every day. As the Savior of the world, he is most alluring, captivating, and compelling. None can compare to him. And he does not rely on the physical beauty for this magnetism; he relies on the spiritual, the eternal, and the everlasting.

The beauty of the Lord is truly lasting beauty! And in it is no vanity at all.

Time to think about it

What is God revealing to me through today's devotion?

_____

_____

_____

_____

What is one specific thing I can do to apply this lesson to my life?

_____

_____

_____

_____

DAY 18: BEAUTY IS IN THE EYES OF THE BEHOLDER

> But the Lord said unto Samuel, Look not on his countenance, or on the height of his stature; because I have refused him: for the Lord seeth not as man seeth; for man looketh on the outward appearance, but the Lord looketh on the heart.
>
> 1 Samuel 16:7

Beauty is such a subjective thing. What one person admires as flawless and exquisite, another sees as flawed and unattractive. We all have our individual tastes, our likes and dislikes, but one thing we know for certain, no matter what a person looks like on the outside, God is neither impressed nor repulsed. The Great Creator in heaven made us all in his image, fearfully and wonderfully so! He is the Potter who molds many vessels and places them on a shelf. They are all of different sizes, shapes, and colors. Some are smooth; some are textured. They are unique, and yes, some may be prettier than others in the natural eyes of man, but to the Potter, they are all beautiful and a choice reflection of his hands. The Potter knows that the true value of each piece rests in the heart of the vessel. He looks down upon them from his place of sovereignty and peers deeply within. He sees the potential that lies inside these vessels, waiting to be used by him. The outward beauty is inconsequential. Can the vessel hold? Can it serve? Is it useful? Is it worthy of the Master's gifts? These are the questions to ask.

When I was a teenager, I had a crush on a guy whom Ma Dear thought was unattractive. She pointed out his every flaw: his wide nose, the pimples on his face, his extremely bowed legs, and his much-too-wide, boyish grin. She finally told me, "Well, I guess beauty is in the eyes of the beholder." I remember her dismissive gaze—perched lips and eyes peering at me from her slightly bowed and tilted head. "I just don't like the way he looks!" she would say with a grin. Merely looking upon his physical presentation, she did not see anything to be desired. He was not tall. He was not handsome. And she would have refused him, finding him lacking. Oh, aren't we *blessed* that God does not measure us in such a way? Our God in heaven looks beyond our physical presentation, and with his all-seeing and righteous eyes, he lovingly beholds each of us as possessing a spiritual beauty.

Time to think about it

What is God revealing to me through today's devotion?

_____

_____

_____

_____

What is one specific thing I can do to apply this lesson to my life?

_____

_____

_____

_____

DAY 19: DON'T BURN YOUR BRIDGES AFTER YOU CROSS THEM

> Likewise, ye younger, submit yourselves unto the elder. Yea, all of you be subject one to another, and be clothed with humility: for God resisteth the proud, and giveth grace to the humble.
>
> 1 Peter 5:5

Pride will lead a person to do strange things. And more often than not, it causes permanent damage to relationships, burning those metaphorical bridges and leaving piles of ashes that cannot be crossed again. The problem, however, with burning those bridges is that one never *truly* knows for certain when or if he will need them again. So I ask the question, why let pride keep you from making amends with those who have offended you or whom you have offended?

The prodigal son, whom Jesus teaches about (see Luke 15), had to swallow his pride and return home. Having gone to his father and asked for the portion of goods that he would later inherit, he took his money and left home. He went out and had a good time, spending and "wast[ing] his substance with riotous living" (v. 13 KJV). I'm sure that when he left home, he never imagined that the day would come when he would have to return there to seek refuge from the storms of life. However, that is exactly what happened. When a mighty famine arose in the land (v. 14 KJV), the young man found himself in dire need. In fact, he was in such a state that the Bible tells us he would have gladly eaten the husks that were fed to the pigs (v. 16 KJV). All of his money was gone, and his friends took the first flight out with the money. It was in his favor that his father loved him and had a heart of forgiveness. The father could have stood before the ashes of a bridge burnt to the ground by his son's actions, but he didn't. Instead, while the son was away, the father stood watch over the bridge. I like to think of this particular bridge as a drawbridge, one that had been pulled in for a season, but when the need arises, it can be let down in order for the son to cross back over it, to home.

That's how our Heavenly Father is with us. Sometimes, we veer off from the path, for "all we like sheep have gone astray" (Isaiah 63:6 KJV). But God, in his love and compassion, allowed his Son to become a bridge bearing our iniquities so that we might freely return home. Our Lord, faithful and just, is always there to forgive us of our sins if we come to him with a sincere heart and confess before him (see I John 1:9).

Time to think about it

What is God revealing to me through today's devotion?

_____

_____

_____

_____

What is one specific thing I can do to apply this lesson to my life?

_____

_____

_____

_____

DAY 20: BLIND IN ONE EYE AND CAN'T SEE OUT OF THE OTHER

> Having the understanding darkened, being alienated from the life of God through the ignorance that is in them, because of the blindness of their heart.
>
> Ephesians 4:18

Sometimes in life, the things of God escape us, particularly when we attempt to understand spiritual things through carnal thinking. We, with our finite minds, are oblivious to His will unless our gracious Father in heaven reveals it to us. Why? It is because the truths of God are spiritual and must be discerned with a spiritual mind. We cannot approach the things of God via the veil of carnality. We must allow the Spirit to lead, guide, and direct us and allow it to reveal these things to us when the time comes. The beauty of placing our trust in God's plan of revelation is that "The Lord is not slack concerning his promise,…[and] not willing that any should perish, but that all should come to repentance" (2 Peter 3:9). The Lord wants all of his sons and daughters to see *and* see through his eyes.

However, those who live in sin cannot perceive the things of God. They are "[e]ver learning, and never able to come to the knowledge of the truth" (2 Timothy 3:7). Truth must be revealed to them by God or taught to them by someone sent by God. In Acts 8, the Ethiopian eunuch sat in his chariot, reading the Word of God, but he did not understand it. The Spirit of the Lord *sent* Philip to the eunuch to guide him through the scripture. When the man of God expounded the Word to the eunuch and preached Jesus unto him, his life was changed. The Bible declares that "if our gospel be hid, it is hid to them that are lost: In whom the god of this world hath blinded the minds of them which believe not" (2 Cor. 4:3–4). When that unbelieving soul finally comes to believe, his faith tills the soil of his heart so that God's eternal truths may take root and began a change in his life. Then he is able to *see* clearly.

> But as it is written, Eye hath not seen, nor ear heard, neither have entered into the heart of man, the things which God hath prepared for them that love him. *But God hath revealed them unto us by his Spirit* (emphasis mine): for the Spirit searcheth all things, yea, the deep things of God. For what man knowth the things of a man, save the spirit of man which is in him? even so the things of God knoweth no man, but the Spirit of God. Now we have received, not the spirit of the world, but the spirit which

is of God; that we might know the things that
are freely given to us of God.

1 Corinthians 2:9–12 KJV

When Jesus's disciples wanted to know why he spoke in parables, Jesus replied, "Because it is given unto you to know the mysteries of the kingdom of heaven, but to them it is not given" (Matthew 13:11 KJV). Praise God for being a part of his family, for membership has its privileges: the divine revelation of his word, the blessed impartation of his Spirit, knowledge and understanding of his will, and his inexplicable power and grace to walk in both. We are not blind—having eyes to see but refusing to see. Instead, "We *know* that the Son of God is come, and hath *given us an understanding*, that *we may know him* that is true, and we are in him that is true, even in his Son Jesus Christ. This is the true God, and eternal life" (1 John 5:20 KJV [emphasis mine]). Be blessed in the knowledge of God, having opened eyes that are not blind to his truths.

Time to think about it

What is God revealing to me through today's devotion?

___

___

___

___

What is one specific thing I can do to apply this lesson to my life?

_____

_____

_____

_____

DAY 21:
IT'S SIX IN ONE HAND AND HALF A DOZEN IN THE OTHER

> Whether is easier, to say, Thy sins be forgiven thee; or to say, Rise up and walk?
>
> Luke 5:23

When faced with choices in life that yielded comparable outcomes, my Ma Dear would say, "Doesn't matter… six in one hand and half a dozen in the other!" In other words, she would be just as pleased—or displeased—with either result. In this world we live in, we are often presented with such decisions to make. I know I am and on a daily basis. Should I take Interstate 10 as my route to church or travel Highway 290? Both will likely have construction work in progress, impeding my getting to church on time. Then after church on Sundays, my husband always asks me where do I want to go for dinner, and every Sunday, the answer is the same—it doesn't matter. I usually don't have a preference and would prefer if he, the finicky eater, selected a place. What's more important to me is, should I have peach cobbler or banana pudding for dessert? Either, however, will likely land me in the gym for an extra thirty minutes on the treadmill. Oh well. Making such decisions can be most difficult. How does one choose between two highly desirable options or select one of two loathsome tasks? I'm glad that not all choices are like this.

When it comes to obeying God, our decisions become clearer and much more impactful. The word is close to us, placed on a table within reach. God says, "See, I have set before thee this day life and good, and death and evil" (Deuteronomy 30:15). Our job is to choose wisely, and it is not a very difficult decision to make because the expected outcomes are not comparable in the least. Serve God and live; serve his enemy and die. Love God and cleave to him; love his enemy and reap eternal damnation. There's no comparison.

In Luke 5, Jesus performed a miracle, and in doing so, he made a choice. While Jesus was teaching among the Pharisees and doctors of the law one day, some men brought in a man lying in his bed, stricken with palsy. They couldn't get through the crowd and had to lower the man from the rooftop into the presence of Jesus that the man might be healed by the Great Physician. When Jesus saw the faith of these men, he spoke to the one who was ill and said, "Man, thy sins are forgiven thee" (v. 20 KJV). Immediately, the scribes and Pharisees began to think—or reason within themselves—accusations of blasphemy against Jesus for indicating that he had the power to forgive sins. The Master, in his omniscience, perceived their very thoughts and asked, "Whether is easier, to say, Thy sins be forgiven thee;

or to say, Rise up and walk?" (Luke 5:23 KJV). Both were in his power, and their outcomes were the same; deliverance had come! It was for *their* benefit that Jesus spoke forgiveness of sin! Then he turned to the man who was sick and told him to "Arise, and take up thy couch, and go into thine house" (v. 24 KJV), and the Bible tells us that immediately, the man did as Jesus instructed and glorified God. The scribes and Pharisees were left to be witnesses. The Son of God spoke healing, and healing happened, so when he spoke forgiveness to the man's sins, forgiveness happened as well. Jesus knew that whatever he spoke, it would come to pass and the man would be made whole, but he wanted the Pharisees to see and know his full authority on earth.

Time to think about it

What is God revealing to me through today's devotion?

_____

_____

_____

_____

What is one specific thing I can do to apply this lesson to my life?

_____

_____

_____

_____

DAY 22: BLOOD IS THICKER THAN WATER

> As we have therefore opportunity, let us do good unto all men, especially unto them who are of the household of faith.
>
> Galatians 6:10 kjv

> For whosoever shall do the will of my Father which is in heaven, the same is my brother, and sister, and mother.
>
> Matthew 12:50 kjv

There is no denying that family is important. God blesses us here on earth with family members to help us in times of need and to rejoice with us in times of gladness. God gives us special people to love us and be loved by us. I also believe that it is through our love for family that we get a glimpse of God's love, that we can, in some small way, understand what love is all about. Nevertheless, family is not limited to those who are blood relatives only. Family represents those people in our lives who love us and are there for us, whether they be kin to us by blood or not. For example, I have a father whom I did not meet or know until I was fourteen years old. Throughout my life, I can count on one hand the number of times I have seen him. I may share similar strands of DNA; his blood may course through my veins, and I may even share his blood type—who knows?—but that alone does not make us family, not in the true sense of the word. On the other hand, my stepfather and my father-in-law are men who entered my life in my late teens and early twenties respectively. They have both been there to offer me advice, care and concern, support, and understanding. I have laughed with them and cried with them. For that reason, the expression "Blood is thicker than water" must hold some *other* truth.

The original meaning of the expression is "The blood of the covenant is thicker than the water of the womb" (from "'How Shall I Know?' The Blood Covenant" by R. Richard Pustelniak). Our utmost loyalty rests in doing the will of God and doing good—according to God's will—unto all men, but especially those who are of the household of faith. Jesus said, "For whosoever shall do the will of my Father which is in heaven, the same is my brother, and sister, and mother" (Matthew 12:50 KJV). We have been adopted into the Royal Family of heaven and are heirs of the Most High God, joint heirs with his Son, Jesus (see Romans 8:17).

Yes, blood is definitely thicker than water, but it is the *blood of Jesus* to which this phrase applies. It is the blood of Jesus that cleanses us of our sins, washes us, and makes us clean. It is the blood of Jesus that binds us together and engrafts us into that royal priesthood.

It is the blood of Jesus that is thicker than any water of the human womb.

Time to think about it

What is God revealing to me through today's devotion?

_____

_____

_____

_____

What is one specific thing I can do to apply this lesson to my life?

_____

_____

_____

_____

DAY 23: CAN'T SEE THE FOREST FOR THE TREES

> You blind fools! Which is greater: the gold, or the temple that makes the gold sacred?…You blind men! Which is greater: the gift, or the altar that makes the gift sacred?
>
> Matthew 23:17 and 19 NIV

> Woe to you, teachers of the law and Pharisees, you hypocrites! You give a tenth of your spices—mint, dill and cumin. But you have neglected the more important matters of the law—justice, mercy and faithfulness. You should have practiced the latter, without neglecting the former. You blind guides! You strain out a gnat but swallow a camel.
>
> Matthew 23:23–24 NIV

Our God works in stages. He did it with Abraham, who left his home, not knowing where he was going. He did it again with Abraham who was told to offer his promised child as an offering to God. Abraham was prepared to slay his son on the altar, trusting that God would raise him up again. God did it with Jacob, who became father of the children of Israel. He also did it with Joseph, who said to his brothers who sold him into slavery. "Now therefore be not grieved, nor angry with yourselves, that ye sold me hither: for *God did send me* before you to preserve life" (Genesis 45:5 KJV [emphasis mine]). God also worked in stages with Queen Esther, who was asked the question, "and who knoweth whether thou art come to the kingdom for such a time as this?" (Esther 4:14 KJV). Many in the Bible saw only part of the whole and walked by faith one step at a time, trusting that each tree revealed the forest of God surrounding them.

When I lived in Atlanta, Georgia, during the late '80s and early '90s, I worked for a large insurance company for about four years—first as a claims coder and then as a marketing assistant. While working in the marketing department, I assisted the national accounts' sales and service representatives and the manager of the department. I was the administrative support, responsible for typing their correspondence, answering phone calls when they were out, resolving minor service issues, and assisting with rate proposals for prospective clients. I enjoyed my work and took pride in my organization. I also liked that I was able to interact with other departments within the company, such as underwriting and legal.

After working in this position for about a year, I began to notice changes in the department. It started with the sales representative leaving for maternity leave. In addition to my own responsibilities, I then had to handle the bulk of her duties as well. A few months later, the service representative became pregnant, and she too decided to leave. Initially I thought, "No big deal! I can run interference for our accounts until they find a replacement for her." So I took on the service rep's duties as well. However, soon afterward came my whining and complaining: I was performing their work but not making their money; I was only one person, doing the work of three. Growing tired from the added responsibilities, I was more than a little relieved when some of the sales and service reps' duties were transferred to a national accounts claims unit two floors up. Then one day, the manager of my department announced that she was being transferred to an office in another city in Georgia, and she would be performing most of her duties from there for an indefinite amount of time. All of a sudden, I found myself on a job with nothing to do, working in a department that was ceasing to exist more and more each day. Right before my eyes, while pruning the branches of my trees, my forest was being chopped down. I then stood before a shrinking grove with a life-changing decision to make—quit or wait to be laid off.

People have the tendency to view the parade called life from the ground level, only seeing one float, one marching band, or one car passing at a time. There are a select few who get to watch the parade from a rooftop, taking in a little more of the line up at once. There are very few—if any—who get to watch the parade from start to finish in one sweeping glance. Only God's eyes and man's hindsight provide such a bird's-eye view. However, it is our trust in God that allows us to live in his will and know in our hearts that even though we can't see the forest, it is there. Even though we can't see the purpose, there is one. Even though we can't understand the why, God knows, and he will reveal it to us in his time, that God might be glorified!

Time to think about it

What is God revealing to me through today's devotion?

_____

_____

_____

_____

What is one specific thing I can do to apply this lesson to my life?

_____

_____

_____

_____

DAY 24: CAUGHT BETWEEN A ROCK AND A HARD PLACE

> And Moses said unto the people, Fear ye not, stand still, and see the salvation of the Lord, which he will shew to you today: for the Egyptians whom ye have seen today, ye shall see them again no more fore ever. The Lord shall fight for you, and ye shall hold your peace.
>
> Exodus 14:13–14 KJV

There have been times in my life when I was faced with a decision to make, and neither option A nor option B presented something I really wanted to do. Usually, it was a choice between hurting someone else or hurting myself. Before I met my husband, the choice would have been easy—hurt myself and keep the peace. However, once Greg came along, I then had this stubborn man in my corner, loving me and looking out for me. No matter what was going on, he never heeded my pleas to just let me handle it, but he would always step in and would not allow me to sacrifice my own happiness for the happiness of others. Of course, I realized that he was only trying to help, but boy did he put me in an uncomfortable place—the place of having to say no to my family. It was during those times—stuck between my family and my husband—that I found myself calling out to God because I didn't know what to do. Over and over again, the Lord was faithful for he heard my cries and intervened on my behalf. He either fixed the problem so that I didn't have to do anything (praise God!), or he gave me strength to stand up for myself and not give in to the demands of others just to keep them happy with me.

When God's people find themselves at the Red Sea and under hot pursuit of Pharaoh's army, or when they find themselves adrift between Scylla and Charybdis, the appropriate course of action lies in the pages of God's Word. If we would only call on the Lord, he will not fail us in our times of trouble. Psalm 18:6 KJV says, "In my distress I called upon the Lord, and cried unto my God: he heard my voice out of his temple, and my cry came before him, even into his ears." What a blessed people we are to have a God who hears us when we call. He is a mighty fortress and strong tower in which the saints of God may run for safety and refuge. God will fight the battle if we allow him to, for the battle belongs to him anyway. I certainly would not want to be the one who wages war against a saint of God for God is the saint's protector. He declares in Isaiah 41:10 KJV, "[F]ear not, for I am with you; be not dismayed, for I am your God; I will strengthen you, I will help you, I will uphold you with my righteous right hand." With a promise like that, our success is inevitable and our rescue assured.

The Bible says, "God is our refuge and strength, a very present help in trouble" (Psalm 46:1 KJV). Stand on his word. Don't let trouble paralyze you with dread, causing you to fear what lies to the left and to the right. Don't let the trials of life lodge you between two undesirables. Look to the Lord, the author and finisher of your faith, who will bring you out. Look to him who will deliver you from the snare of the enemy. Speak to yourself the promises of God that "[n]o weapon that is formed against thee shall prosper; and every tongue that shall rise against thee in judgment thou shalt condemn. This is the heritage of all God's servants" (Isaiah 54:17). And he will be with you always.

Time to think about it

What is God revealing to me through today's devotion?

_____

_____

_____

_____

What is one specific thing I can do to apply this lesson to my life?

_____

_____

_____

_____

DAY 25: CLOTHES DON'T MAKE THE MAN

> And why do you worry about clothes? See how the flowers of the field grow. They do not labor or spin. Yet I tell you that not even Solomon in all his splendor was dressed like one of these.
>
> Matthew 6:28–29, NIV

Today, we live in a world where outward appearances are highly valued. One only has to turn on the television, log on to the internet, or open a magazine to see where the ideals of society lie. Instead of desiring a heart like Christ's, some women desire a body like Beyonce's. Instead of the temperance and patience seen in a meek and quiet spirit, some are seeking fame and fortune in a materialistic world. Instead of seeking an upright walk with Christ, many are striving for a *tight whip* with rims. We have convinced ourselves that the best way to measure a man's success is by what he wears on his body or flashes on his arm. For this reason, top names in the fashion industry have become household names. Sporting the latest from Dolce and Gabbana or Michael Kor has become *en vogue*. If the celebrities are wearing it or carrying it, then it must be the new standard of dress. And so off we go, seeking the materialism, acceptance, and approval of this world.

How can this be when Jesus clearly told his followers that their bodies are *more than raiment* (see Matthew 6:25), meaning their bodies have a greater purpose in the kingdom than that of a clothes rack. Okay, let me pause here and state that I'm not suggesting that Christians walk around looking homely or unkempt. We are, after all, children of the King. However, our clothes should not be our primary focus when it comes to what we want others to see in (not on) us. How are we presenting ourselves as agents of the Lord?

I remember when I was in middle school and high school, Ma Dear often sewed our clothes. As a middle school student, my choir uniform was the standout! My baby blue skirt was made with gathers, while all the other girls' skirts were A-line. Even the fabric was different in color and texture because my grandmother bought what she could afford. My navy vest to the uniform was made of plush velour, while the other girls' vests were made of the knit material selected by our choir instructor. There were many times I felt awkward about my attire because I was wearing something homemade—and usually a little quirky—because Ma Dear loved incorporating her uniqueness into her work. My slacks closed with Velcro because she thought it was *neat*—no button holes. My blouses had crazy swirls and psychedelic patterns in the fabric because she loved the loud, moving colors—the last thing, by the way, in which a teenager wants to be seen. The fit of the garments was usually off as well. My sophomore year in school, she made me a pair of red gabardine pants that were too big in the hips. She instantly sensed my concern about the excess fabric because I kept tugging at the fabric around my hips. She told me not to worry about it because the extra fabric made my pants resemble the riding pants that jockeys wore. She even pointed out the extra-wide waistband that gave the slacks a tuxedo-pants look, having a built-in cummerbund. Simply put, Ma Dear created her own unique clothing line and used *me* as her runway model. I say *me* because my sister often left her originally designed pieces hanging in her closet, but I just couldn't do it. I was always aware that no matter how strange I looked, Ma Dear was doing the best she could, and I was careful not to hurt her feelings over anything she sewed for me. So I wore every piece. What I learned in doing so is that I had to find something *inside of me* to reaffirm who I was. I couldn't rely on what I was wearing to make me special—not in the way I wanted—or give me pride, dignity, self-respect, or self-esteem. I had to draw those things from within, and I'm grateful for that today.

I have learned that stressing or worrying about what we are wearing, trying to keep up with the latest fashions, and going broke for the sake of our wardrobe should not be named among the children of God. Jesus discouraged such behavior. He told us *not to worry* about these things, "For the pagans run after all these things, and your heavenly Father knows that you need them" (Matthew 6:32 NIV). We can rest assured that the Lord will provide our needs, and he will clothe us in humility and appropriately adorn us as vessels of righteousness. Instead of seeking better and greater garments to decorate this flesh, let us "seek…first the kingdom of God, and his righteousness; and all these things shall be added" (Matthew 6:33 KJV). Clothes do not make the man or woman. It is what you're *made of*—that inward adornment—that determines who or what you are in Christ Jesus. Let's always keep in mind that "[m]an looks on the outward appearance, but God looks on the heart" (1 Samuel 16:7 KJV), and let us always seek to please God.

Time to think about it

What is God revealing to me through today's devotion?

_____

_____

_____

_____

What is one specific thing I can do to apply this lesson to my life?

_____

_____

_____

_____

DAY 26: EXPERIENCE IS THE BEST TEACHER

> I thought to myself, "Look, I have grown and increased in wisdom more than anyone who has ruled over Jerusalem before me; I have experienced much of wisdom and knowledge."
>
> Ecclesiastes 1:16 NIV

There are some things in life that must be learned by practicing: cooking, driving, swimming, teaching, reading, and the list goes on. You don't just learn these things by reading a book, but you must practice them, engage in them, and *do* them. These are those things in life for which there are no shortcuts or substitutions. You just have to buckle down and master them through flat-footed, bold-faced, and courageous confrontation. When faced with *life* and its most meaningful lessons, its most difficult tasks, and its many duties, experience is the best teacher, and in my life, marriage has been the perfect classroom!

I married my husband on June 27, 1987. I was young, in love, and ever so hopeful. At that time, I could not imagine that life with this man would be anything less than perfect, *all the time*. After all, I loved him, and he loved me. We had passion and desire for one another, and we were enraptured whenever we were in each other's presence. Such feelings would get us through *anything*, and we believed that there was nothing before us that was insurmountable. We could leap small buildings in a single bound as long as we were leaping them together, holding hands. Then suddenly, the spinning wheel of life stopped on the space-marked challenges. Conflicts and differences of opinions arose in paradise, and it was only a matter of time before the flaming swords signaled our stay in Eden was over. What on earth were we to do?

Part of the problem was our different backgrounds. When I married, my mother was twice divorced; her mother was divorced and never remarried. I came from an environment where marital bliss did not reside, while my husband came from an environment where he had the ideal marriage as his example. This Cleaver home was what he wanted and expected from our marriage, and June Cleaver I was not. To be honest, he wasn't exactly Ward. So my experience regarding marriage left much to be desired, and his experience was a tad unrealistic with me as a wife. Still, it was my prayer that God would help me to be a wife according to his word, that he help me to submit to my own husband, that he help me to be chaste and a keeper at home, rearing my children in the fear and admonition of the Lord, creating a loving home of peace and joy. It was a tall order, but I found that nothing is too hard for God, and he blessed my marriage and my home, teaching me through the experiences in my marriage.

Through living God's word concerning man and woman on a daily basis, our marriages can be blessed. By showing up for class every day and being willing to put in the time and effort to learn and do well, we become successful pupils. Glory to God! Experience will show us the value and importance of always laughing and communicating with one another. Experience will teach us to put the needs of our spouse above our own that we might live in harmony and peace. Experience will teach and reveal those tiny idiosyncrasies that make each of us unique and interesting but also sometimes difficult to live with. Experience will teach us to identify those moments when it is okay to broach a particular topic and when it is best to let it lie for a while. From living with someone, you experience them, and that experience is the best way to get to know them.

It has only been through my showing up for class every day for the last twenty-seven years that I have come to know my husband and be his help. God said in Genesis 2:18 and 24 KJV, "And the LORD God said, It is not good that the man should be alone; I will make him an help meet for him.... Therefore shall a man leave his father and his mother, and shall cleave unto his wife: and they shall be one flesh." It is one thing to read these words on a page, but until we put them into practice and really live them within the sanctity of marriage, they have little meaning. This thing called marriage is a permanent covenant and a lifetime commitment to merge your life with another person's. In this merging, we get an idea of the church's preparation for her marriage to the Lamb. Matthew 19:6 (KJV) says, "Wherefore they are no more twain, but one flesh. What therefore God hath joined together, let not man put asunder." Experience has taught me that one of the major problems facing marriages today is that both partners are trying to maintain their separation within the union. This is a recipe for failure. There is no more two but both must yield themselves to becoming one. That's God's way, the only way.

Time to think about it

What is God revealing to me through today's devotion?

_____

_____

_____

_____

What is one specific thing I can do to apply this lesson to my life?

_____

_____

_____

_____

DAY 27: GOD HELPS THOSE WHO HELP THEMSELVES

> For as the body without the spirit is dead, so faith without works is dead also.
>
> James 2:26 KJV

God will also help those who are unable to help themselves, but I get the point. If I make one step, then the Lord will make two. In other words, God will honor effort. It is easy to fall for that false assumption that when we trust God, we should sit back and do nothing and wait for him to work a miracle. Can the Lord make your telephone ring with employers calling to offer you the job of a lifetime without some legwork and effort on your part? Absolutely! Will he? Probably not, "for faith without works is dead. Show me your faith without works, and I will show you my faith *by* my works," (see James 2:18 KJV, [emphasis mine]). I am also instantly reminded of the Moabite woman Ruth, a daughter of God who received honor for her act of faith and the initiative she displayed. Ruth did not just sit around, waiting for things to happen. She stepped out and did something about her situation, and God moved in a mighty way, rewarding her effort.

Ruth's story took place during the days when the judges ruled in Israel. A man named Elimelech moved to Moab with his wife Naomi and their two sons Mahlon and Chilion. Then Elimelech died and left Naomi and her two sons who married two Moabite girls, Orpah and Ruth. After a number of years, the sons died also, leaving Naomi and her daughters-in-law alone. Deciding to return to her home, Naomi instructed Orpah and Ruth to return to their mothers' homes for she had no more sons for husbands. In tears, Orpah returned home, but Ruth "clave unto [Naomi]" (Ruth 1:14 KJV) and returned with her to Bethlehem "in the beginning of barley harvest" (v. 22 KJV).

Finding themselves near dire straits, Ruth went into the field of Naomi's wealthy kinsman, Boaz, to glean after the reapers so that she and Naomi might have food to eat. In her initiative, Ruth attracted the attention and favor of Boaz who welcomed her with kindness and generosity. When Ruth asked him why he was so kind to her, a stranger, Boaz first acknowledged Ruth's own kindness to Naomi and then replied, "The LORD recompense thy work, and a full reward be given thee of the LORD God of Israel, under whose wings thou art come to trust" (Ruth 2:12 KJV). Ruth's trust was in the God of Israel, and when she moved according to his will, he blessed her abundantly. In the end, Ruth became the wife of Boaz, the mother of Obed, the grandmother of Jesse, and the great grandmother of

King David. Because she was willing to help herself, God blessed her efforts and came quickly to her rescue.

Time to think about it

What is God revealing to me through today's devotion?

_____

_____

_____

_____

What is one specific thing I can do to apply this lesson to my life?

_____

_____

_____

_____

DAY 28: GOD MOVES IN MYSTERIOUS WAYS

> For as the heavens are higher than the earth, so are my ways higher than your ways, and my thoughts than your thoughts.
>
> Isaiah 55:9 kjv

Have you ever found yourself asking the question(s), "Why did God allow this?" or "Why did God do such and such that way?" I know I have; I've sat in silence and wonder, pondering the ways of God. Of course, it is all to no avail because our minds are finite, trying to decipher an infinite God. His ways are higher than our ways, and his thoughts certainly supersede our tiny thoughts (see Isaiah 55:8-9 kjv). Who can ever know him and the thoughts of his mind?

When I was a teenager, I was betrayed and deeply hurt by a close family friend. It completely blindsided me, leaving me devastated and disillusioned. For many years afterward, I kept the experience folded in blankets of shame, and I tucked it away in a closet of denial. When I took the time to revisit the memory, I always struggled with figuring out *why*.

In essence, I found myself sounding a little like Job and his friends, trying to determine why painful and senseless things happen to us. After Job and his friends had their say, the Lord God of heaven spoke to Job himself. Even now, my eyes flood as I read but a small portion of God's questioning of Job:

> *Where wast thou* when I laid the foundations of the earth? declare, *if thou hast understanding.* Who hath laid the measures thereof, *if thou knowest*? or who hath stretched the line upon it? Whereupon are the foundations thereof fastened? or who laid the corner stone thereof; When the morning stars sang together, and all the sons of God shouted for joy? Or who shut up the sea with doors, when it brake forth, as if it had issued out of the womb?…Hast thou commanded the morning since thy days; and caused the dayspring to know his place.
>
> Job 38:4–8 and 12 KJV (emphasis mine)

Of course, the answers are *nowhere, no, sir,* and *I don't know.* We were merely a thought at that time, knowing nothing, existing only in the mind of the Most High. As human beings, we may never understand it all, especially the meaning behind loss and hurt and pain and suffering, "[for] who hath known the mind of the Lord? or who can be his counselor?" (Romans 11:34 KJV); nevertheless, we can always depend on the God of our salvation to be merciful and kind and loving toward each of us in the healing. We can always trust him to bring peace and restoration, joy and resolution—but in his own time. The Word declares, "how unsearchable are his judgments, and his ways past finding out!" (Romans 11:33 KJV). Still, we can trust him!

As for me, I never figured out the reason that drove this trusted family friend to hurt me. Those are mere excuses I will never know. However, I have learned this: I would never know that God can heal the deepest of lacerations had I not been deeply cut. I would never know the extent to which God can calm the greatest fear had I not known terror. I would never know that God can take away the most agonizing pain had I not been tossed in agony. And I would never know that God can dry the greatest ocean had I not cried one myself too many nights. Sadly, the testimony can only follow the test. We may not always understand why God allows certain things to happen to us, but we can always be certain that if he allows us to come to a fire, it is never for the purpose of consuming us, but he wants to bring us through the flames—glorifying him.

Time to think about it

What is God revealing to me through today's devotion?

_____

_____

_____

_____

What is one specific thing I can do to apply this lesson to my life?

_____

_____

_____

_____

DAY 29: YOU'RE JUMPING OUT OF THE FRYING PAN AND INTO THE FIRE

> [F]or I have learned, in whatsoever state I am, therewith to be content.
>
> Philippians 4:11b KJV

When our backs are against the wall, the best thing we can do is simply *stand still and see the salvation of the Lord* (see 2 Chronicles 20:17 KJV). Seriously, seek God through prayer, fasting, and daily meditation in his Word, and move *only* when God says go. To do otherwise, my friend, may lead you from the discomfort of the frying pan straight into the destruction of the fire beneath. Yes, it is dangerous in the frying pan for the flames underneath are heating things up in your life to an unbearable degree. Things may seem to be chaotic: children are disobedient, the spouse is insensitive, your finances aren't as you would like them, *this* is broken, and *that* needs fixing. Peace has given way to despair, and hope is hiding out. However, the barrier of the pan that holds you and your troubles should not be taken lightly. As long as you remain there, there is a chance that help will come and lift you from the troubles that surround you. However, if you give up and remove yourself from the situation, you gamble, not knowing if the alternative is better or worse.

Although this is not as drastic as the fires of life, I am often tempted to move from the slow to the fast when I'm in a hurry. My eyes dart from one situation to another in search of the better, the faster, and the easier. For example, standing in one check-out line at the grocery store, I find myself eyeing the next one to see if it is moving faster. After driving up to an ATM, I always notice when another lane becomes free first. When driving down the highway in the fast lane, I am overly cognizant of the fact that the slow lane moves forward more briskly. Then I jump in that lane only to see the fast lane now speeding ahead of me. It never fails! Even in this, we must learn the lessons of patience and contentment.

The apostle Paul was definitely on to something huge and valuable for inner peace when he stated, "for I have learned, in whatsoever state I am, therewith to be content" (Philippians 4:11b KJV). Sometimes, we can be in too much of a hurry to change things and to rid ourselves of discomfort, and we end up missing out on opportunities to learn and grow from the tests we have been given. Allow God to settle your spirit today, and accept the place where he has placed you. Seek to know, grow, and learn from it. And while you are there, seek his presence that it might overshadow you. Seek his will for your life that you might know it completely before making a move. "Trust in the LORD with all thine heart; and lean not unto thine own understanding. In all thy ways acknowledge him, and he shall direct thy paths" (Proverbs 3:5–6 KJV). It is quite possible that doing so could mean the difference between hopping around on your tiptoes in a heated pan and burning to a crisp in an open flame.

Time to think about it

What is God revealing to me through today's devotion?

_____

_____

_____

_____

What is one specific thing I can do to apply this lesson to my life?

_____

_____

_____

_____

DAY 30: DON'T COUNT YOUR CHICKENS BEFORE THEY HATCH

> Some trust in chariots, and some in horses: but we will remember the name of the LORD our God.
>
> Psalm 20:7 KJV

Have you ever spent the check before it actually arrived in the mail? Have you ever spoken a word before you had all the facts? Made a promise before having the provisions to keep it? Have you ever made plans without consulting the Master for his approval? Have you ever relied on someone else to come through so that you could deliver on your end, and the person you were relying on dropped the ball? Have you ever trusted *yourself* to do something, or have you ever agreed to do something but later found the task beyond your ability, or willingness to complete? Most of us, at one time or another, have been guilty of counting those chicks and banking on them before they were actually hatched from the shells. It is no wonder the Bible says to us, "He that trusteth in his own heart is a fool: but whoso walketh wisely, he shall be delivered" (Proverbs 28:26 KJV).

We cannot know the future or what tomorrow plans to bring our way. James 4:14–15 says it plainly: "Whereas ye know not what shall be on the morrow. For what is your life? It is even a vapour, that appeareth for a little time, and then vanisheth away, For that ye ought to say, If the Lord will, we shall live, and do this, or that" (KJV). But wait a minute, isn't it simply an *act of faith* to step out on the ledge and trust God to come through? Well, it could be. However, one must seriously examine his or her motives in such cases. Are you tempting God? Are you trying to impress man by pretending to be more than you are or to have more than you truly possess? Are you, as the Bible says, rejoicing in your boastings (v. 16 KJV)? All such motives and all such rejoicing are evil (v. 16 KJV) in the sight of God, and he who is led by them lies to himself. God will not honor this tempting of his power.

However, when God has instructed you, his child, to move *in faith*, trusting and depending on the Father to work a miracle that *he*, the Father, might receive glory, then you, as a child of God, must move. By all means, go forth. "Humble your[self] in the sight of the Lord, and he shall lift you up" (James 4:10 KJV). The patriarch Abraham has such a testimony. He was ready and willing to offer his son Isaac as a sacrifice unto his God. He believed in his heart that if he performed the will of God, that God would return his son to him. He did not make an attempt, *hoping* that God would come through. He lifted his hand to slay his only son, *knowing* that God would come through. In such cases, those chickens, though they might be caught in a thicket, are as good as hatched!

Time to think about it

What is God revealing to me through today's devotion?

_____

_____

_____

_____

What is one specific thing I can do to apply this lesson to my life?

_____

_____

_____

_____

DAY 31: BIRDS OF A FEATHER FLOCK TOGETHER

> Can two walk together, except they be agreed?
>
> Amos 3:3 KJV

> Be ye not unequally yoked together with unbelievers: for what fellowship hath righteousness with unrighteousness? And what communion hath light with darkness?
>
> 2 Corinthians 6:17 KJV

> He that walketh with wise men shall be wise: but a companion of fools shall be destroyed.
>
> Proverbs 13:20

It is human nature to gravitate toward those whom we feel are most like us. For that reason, we can usually get a clear picture of ourselves by examining those with whom we spend—and enjoy spending—the majority of our time.

There is perhaps no better place where this behavior is most demonstrated than in school. As an educator, each year, I stand at my door on the first day of school to welcome the one hundred plus new students assigned to my class. Year after year, I watch in curiosity as jocks enter and cluster themselves together, usually in the back of the room. Cheerleaders and drill team members find each other and gather in the center. The overachievers and teacher-pleasers dutifully and predictably sit in the front row, while the underachievers and disinterested gifted claim the perimeter of the room, as far away from the teacher's space as possible. Often, race and ethnicity would play a role in how students group themselves in a classroom if I leave them to assign themselves seating.

Even though I do believe that opposites attract, it is still quite obvious that people tend to seek and find companion in those with whom they have things in common. This creates comfort and allows us to fit in more easily. Because this is true, it is paramount that the children of God stay close to those who are also in the body of Christ. Amos 3:3 (KJV) asks, "Can two walk together, except they be agreed?" Harmony exists when two friends, two coworkers, two family members, a husband and wife, or any two people walk together. This harmony cannot exist when two who do not agree attempt to walk together in agreement. What fellowship has light with darkness? As a believer, the light of Christ that rests in and upon the Christian seeks to pull the unbeliever toward the light. The unbeliever resists the light and seeks to dim it with the darkness of unbelief. These two cannot exist in harmony but will find themselves in a state of perpetual disharmony and paralysis until the weaker of the two surrenders. Peace abides where two agree. Love abides where two agree.

Help and encouragement abide where two agree. And strength abides where two agree.

Do you seek to be wise? Then walk with the wise. Do you seek to show love? Then walk with the one who knows and shows the love of God. Do you want to be patient? Then walk with those who produce the fruit of patience. Do you seek to know Christ intimately? Then walk with those who stay in his presence. Hang out with those who hang out with Jesus! Get in their presence *and his* and stay there. There is no such fellowship or unity of the righteous and the unrighteousness just as oil and water will never mix. Yes, birds of a feather flock together. God intends for us to flock with eagles that we might soar in him.

Time to think about it

What is God revealing to me through today's devotion?

_____

_____

_____

_____

What is one specific thing I can do to apply this lesson to my life?

_____

_____

_____

_____

DAY 32: IF YOU LIE WITH DOGS, YOU'LL GET UP WITH FLEAS

> Beware of dogs, beware of evil workers, beware of the concision. For we are the circumcision, which worship God in the spirit, and rejoice in Christ Jesus, and have no confidence in the flesh
>
> Philippians 3:2–3 KJV

> Can a man take fire in his bosom, and his clothes not be burned?
>
> Proverbs 6:27 KJV

Despite its innuendo, Benjamin Franklin's warning, from *Poor Richard's Almanack*, is forever appropriate, reminding us to be careful of the company we keep. I can hear the voice of Ma Dear warning us, "Everybody is not your friend." Over and over, she encouraged us to be mindful of the people we hung out with because she was a firm believer that birds of a feather flock together. Of course, she saw *her* grandchildren as good and didn't want them corrupted by those other bad seeds. "All it takes," she often said, "is one bad apple to spoil the whole bunch." It's funny. We, ourselves, were little rascals, and I'm sure our friends' parents were probably warning them about us. As an adult looking back on my childhood, I do believe we must choose our running buddies carefully and teach our children to do the same. Apostle Paul writes in 1 Corinthians 15:33 (NIV): "Do not be misled: bad company corrupts good character." So yes, it is important to select friends wisely because "[h]e that walketh with wise men shall be wise; but a companion of fools shall be destroyed" (Proverbs 13:20 KJV).

During my high school years, my best friends and I were inseparable. We walked to school dances and caught rides to football and basketball games together. We met every day after school to go to the youth center where we would hang out and "boy watch." We shared our joys, sorrows, and our deepest secrets with one another. We definitely influenced each other—sometimes for good and sometimes for not so good. What I find intriguing about our relationship is how much we started to behave like one another. We picked up the same gestures and expressions. We began to cackle alike, and even talk alike. People often remarked that we looked alike. I realized that over time, when you spend countless hours with a person, you naturally pick up their habits. It is easy to do, and it is easy not to filter those habits in the process. We pick up the good and the bad. If the friends you associate with most are flea infested, it is only a matter of time before the creepy crawlers make tracks on you as well. Let us watch diligently and encourage one another to keep looking to Jesus, following him in our relationships that we might emulate the Master and find ourselves pleasing in his eyes.

Time to think about it

What is God revealing to me through today's devotion?

_____

_____

_____

_____

What is one specific thing I can do to apply this lesson to my life?

_____

_____

_____

_____

DAY 33: PEOPLE IN GLASSHOUSES SHOULDN'T THROW STONES

Judge not, that ye be not judged.

Matthew 7:1 KJV

Some things in life seem rather simple to me. For example, if it isn't broken, don't fix it; if you dance to the music, then you must pay the piper; if it doesn't fit, don't force it; and if you can't take it in, then don't dish it out. Simple, right? Yet I am amazed by the number of people who would offer up advice, criticism, and debate at the drop of a dime, and yet they cannot receive it themselves. Growing up, I lived a few doors up from the neighborhood bully. His name was Vincent, and he could not take teasing. When playmates teased him, one could see this veil of anger cloak itself around him, and eventually a dam of fury ruptured, and his wrath would be unleashed. Usually, a fist-flailing battle would ensue in the middle of a kickball game, hopscotch, or hide-and-seek. He could not take the teasing, but He was one of the biggest bullies in the neighborhood. It seemed to take him a while to realize that if he didn't like the teasing, perhaps those whom he teased felt the same way. Eventually, after a few fights, Vincent learned that he had to treat others the way he wanted to be treated. Eventually (thank the Lord), he grew up, and because he didn't take teasing too well himself, he stopped teasing others.

I can only imagine what it would be like living in a glasshouse. The occupant would probably tiptoe about, afraid to offend even the nicest of neighbors because of his vulnerability. I imagine that he would be constantly aware that he is unprotected from harm and destruction that could easily shatter his surroundings. In other words, those who live in glass houses are susceptible to quick and easy destruction. Common sense demands that such a one not throw rocks at his neighbors. This same idea applies to other areas of our lives.

Jesus said to a gathering of Pharisees who were condemning a young woman in adultery and desiring to see her stoned to death, "He that is without sin among you, let him first cast a stone at her" (John 8:7 KJV). These religious leaders who gathered to judge and condemn the adulteress were ready to take aim and fire. However, when Jesus stooped and wrote on the ground, something happened—they became shamefully aware of their own imperfections. The criticizers realized that they had no right and were not worthy to condemn another person because they too were in need of the Physician.

As followers of Christ, we must strive to uplift and encourage others, realizing always that by the grace of God, we are forgiven. We must always treat others the way we want to be treated and never serve up a dish that we ourselves cannot stomach.

Time to think about it

What is God revealing to me through today's devotion?

_____

_____

_____

_____

What is one specific thing I can do to apply this lesson to my life?

_____

_____

_____

_____

DAY 34: DON'T BITE THE HAND THAT FEEDS YOU

> Be kind and compassionate to one another, forgiving each other, just as in Christ God forgave you.
>
> Ephesians 4:32 KJV

Arguably one of the most difficult things we Jesus followers have to do in this life is forgive those who have hurt us. The task is twice as hard when the injury occurred while we were in the process of actually helping them. If you have not faced this type of betrayal before, then I hope you never have to. The truth of the matter, however, is that most of us have. Think about it. Have you ever loaned someone money only to have them seemingly forget that they owe you? And they are wearing a new outfit every time you see them. Have you ever gone out of your way to pick someone up and give him or her a ride, but when you need help (s)he is unavailable? Have you ever rescued a friend in trouble only to have that friend get on his feet and treat you as if you don't exist any longer? Of course we can think of countless examples of people taking a big chomp out of an extended hand while it serves them because frankly, we humans can be plain ol' selfish in nature. When these things happen, you have the right to handle that person with a long-handled spoon, protect yourself, and not be taken advantage of again, right? Wrong! No matter how many times your little fingers have been bitten, no matter how many times you've lost blood trying to help someone, it is still better to help, to be a fool for the sake of righteousness than to become hardened at heart.

When Peter asked Jesus how often he should forgive his brother's sin against him, he wanted to know if he should forgive up to seven times. Jesus replied, "I say not unto thee, Until seven times: but, Until seventy times seven" (Matthew 18:22 KJV). I am humbly reminded to forgive others when I think of the number of times I have bitten the hands of Jesus, taking all of his goodness and mercy, squandering it on selfishness and worldly pleasures, yet he forgives me. If we give up on our loved ones and fail to forgive them, then the Lord will not forgive us. We cannot let unforgiveness keep us from the presence of the Lord.

On the flip side of the coin, we must also remember to show our appreciation for others and what they do for us. The Bible instructs that "[if] it be possible, as much as lieth in [us], live peaceably with all men" (Romans 12:18 KJV) and that includes treating them the way we would like to be treated. Offer love and compassion to all.

Romans 12:10 says, "Be devoted to one another in brotherly love. Honor one another above yourselves" (KJV). Don't bite the hands that feed you but respect them and give them thanks, for such hands are the favor of God in your life. And when we extend a hand to someone only to have it snapped or caught in the clutches of sharpened teeth, give thanks for that as well. Let Jesus serve as an example of how we are to love continually, even in the midst of persecution, and let us remember in prayer all who hurt us. Pray, "Father, forgive them, for they do not know what they are doing" (Luke 23:34 KJV).

Time to think about it

What is God revealing to me through today's devotion?

What is one specific thing I can do to apply this lesson to my life?

_____

_____

_____

_____

DAY 35: THE GRASS IS ALWAYS GREENER ON THE OTHER SIDE OF THE FENCE

> And he said unto them, Take heed, and beware of covetousness: for a man's life consisteth not in the abundance of the things which he possesseth.
>
> Luke 12:15 KJV

Standing in my front yard with my feet planted amidst the dry, crackling, browning blades of grass, I glance across the street at my neighbor's lawn. How plush and thick it appears from my side of the street. How rich and deep in color her grass grows. I stand there with wandering eyes, wishing my grass was like hers, desiring the blessing that she has, and weeping over the dying lawn that is spread before me inside my own fence.

We've all been there—that place of covetousness, wanting something someone else has, something that seemed much better, more attractive, or more promising. "Surely, if it were mine, I would be happier," we tell ourselves. The main problem with thinking the grass on the other side of the fence is more desirable or appealing is that it takes our heart and mind away from the grass that we have beneath our own two feet. Here I stand with that which God has given me, yet it yearns for my attention, thirsts for more water, and hungers to be fertilized. I cannot see to its needs because I'm too focused on how it's failing me, never once considering that I too am failing it. I let it go neglected, abused, unappreciated. Many times, while we are seeking what we don't have, we lose sight of what we do. If I would only take time to attend to my lawn, it would yield the same beauty that my neighbor's does. It would grow as lush and as green. It would be as healthy.

Another problem with eyeing the grass on the other side is that we fail to count up the cost. I've heard my husband preach that greener grass often comes with a bigger water bill. When we want what others have, we don't stop to consider what they've sacrificed to gain it. Have they offered up their family time? Have they compromised true love? Have they lost peace and joy? Have they put aside a closer relationship with the Lord? Matthew 6:33 says, "But seek ye first the kingdom of God, and his righteousness; and all these things shall be added unto you" (KJV). When we seek God first, he will surely bless us. His word declares it. And when God blesses us, we can be assured that "[t]he blessing of the Lord, it maketh rich, and he addeth no sorrow with it" (Proverbs 10:22 KJV).

Let us keep our eyes on the right side of the fence, being thankful for, and attentive to, the things with which God has blessed us. If we are faithful over the little we have, God will add to it; He will enlarge our territory. Be grateful and glorify God always.

Time to think about it

What is God revealing to me through today's devotion?

_____

_____

_____

_____

What is one specific thing I can do to apply this lesson to my life?

_____

_____

_____

_____

DAY 36: NEVER LOOK A GIFT HORSE IN THE MOUTH

> Giving thanks always for all things unto God and the Father in the name of our Lord Jesus Christ.
>
> Ephesians 5:20 KJV

How disappointing it is to offer a gift to someone, only to have him or her scrutinize or inspect its quality, question its worth, or belittle it. To see the gift sit unused or ignored shows ungratefulness, and such behavior is unkind. Such behavior equates to looking a gift horse in the mouth, checking for the length of its teeth. People did this long ago to assess the value of the horse. This should never be our attitude. The scripture admonishes us to give thanks for all things. An attitude of gratitude is always in style.

I remember a time I received a purse from a friend for Christmas. The purse was a navy blue bucket-style purse with brown trim. I *loved* that purse; however, I didn't show my appreciation for it. Sadly, I made the giver feel as if I didn't like or value her gift to me at all.

One day, we were at church for choir rehearsal, and I had set the purse down somewhere. In my search for it, I called out, "Has anyone seen my purse? It's a big, unattractive, blue purse." My friend, who was sitting on the back pew, gave me a funny look, but I still didn't realize that I had just insulted a gift she had given me. It just didn't click! When she pointed it out to me later in the car, I was horrified. Even when I think about this today, I am still hurt over my display of ungratefulness. The irony of it all is that I really did love the purse. Would I ever be able to convince my friend of that? No way.

This was probably twenty years ago, and I still feel the moment as if it were yesterday. Most gifts are sincere expressions of love, thoughtfulness, and heart. When someone cares enough to present you with something he or she picks out especially for you, it speaks volumes. It is a priceless gesture. Give God and the gift giver thanks for remembering you. Let them know how much you appreciate it. Failure to do so is hurtful.

Time to think about it

What is God revealing to me through today's devotion?

_____

_____

_____

_____

What is one specific thing I can do to apply this lesson to my life?

_____

_____

_____

_____

DAY 37: EVERY DUCK PRAISES HIS OWN POND

> If thou hast done foolishly in lifting up thyself, or if thou hast thought evil, lay thine hand upon thy mouth.
>
> Proverbs 30:32 KJV

> Every way of a man is right in his own eyes: but the LORD pondereth the hearts.
>
> Proverbs 21:2 KJV

Every duck may praise his own pond, but let's face it, no one likes a braggart. No one likes being in the presence of one who is filled with arrogance and pride or stuck on himself. No one likes being around someone who is always boasting about his or her possessions, good fortunes, perfect children, beautiful home, intellect, or accomplishments. Such people should know they are headed toward loneliness, and the road is long.

In this age of self-promotion, self-esteem, and self-worth, I listen to people exalt themselves on every hand. We see this pride in status updates and clever tweets on social media websites. Everyone has a perfect life, a wonderful marriage, the best children, and a loving home. No one is afraid because everyone has a unique relationship with the Lord, complete with spiritual boldness, determination, a positive attitude, and fairy dust. It gets crazy at times! Then I am reminded of what my grandmother used to say when she caught me prancing in the mirror, singing into a hairbrush, flinging my hair, and smiling at the star before me: "Well, Lord, every duck praises his own pond!"

Don't get me wrong. There is nothing wrong with recognizing that we are beautiful inside and out. We are made in the image and likeness of God, our Father (see Genesis 1:26 KJV). The Bible says that God created our innermost being, that he covered us in our mothers' wombs, and that we are fearfully and wonderfully made (see Psalm 139:13–14 KJV). Yes, we are magnificent creatures, handcrafted by the Master of Creation. However, when we lift ourselves up, especially above others or higher than we should, the Bible calls it foolish and predicts our fall.

An unhealthy or unrealistic sense of one's self is dangerous. Such perceptions may lead to pride and arrogance. On the other end of the spectrum, it may also produce self-doubt and feelings of inadequacy or not being *good enough*. These attitudes often result in issues like bigotry, apathy, immorality, and hatred of others on one side and self-effacement, self-injury, and self-hatred on the other side. Neither extreme offers a place of peace in which the child of God is to rest. We must always pray to God to give us a balanced and healthy self-image whereby we recognize our gifts and talents and also our flaws and weaknesses. This allows us to give our best to God so that he can bless it and use it for his glory. It also allows us to present to him our weaknesses so that he might strengthen us in those areas, which is again an act of service unto him.

Sadly, we seek self-exaltation in other areas of our lives as well: our jobs, our academic achievements, money, friends, and connections. These should not define us, and we must not seek our worth in such temporal things. "We are God's workmanship, created in Christ Jesus to do good works, which God prepared in advance for us to do" (Ephesians 2:10 kjv). We must realize that it's not about us. We are not beautifully created, brilliant, and talented for our own glory but for the glory of God. No one has boasting rights in and of himself, but we must boast only in the Lord, giving him all the glory and honor that is due him for making *us*. You see, he is the author and finisher of our faith (see Hebrew 12:2 kjv). The Bible says that it is he who made us and not we ourselves (see Psalm 100:3 kjv), and all things were made for *his* pleasure (see Revelations 4:11 kjv). Let us not praise our own pond out of vanity or conceit. Let us praise the Lord for the pond he has given us, always remembering to worship the Creator and not the creature. Bless his holy name!

Time to think about it

What is God revealing to me through today's devotion?

_____
_____
_____
_____

What is one specific thing I can do to apply this lesson to my life?

_____
_____
_____
_____

DAY 38: EVERYTHING THAT'S GOOD TO YOU ISN'T GOOD FOR YOU

> For what shall it profit a man, if he shall gain the whole world, and lose his own soul?
>
> Mark 8:36 KJV

> And she that liveth in pleasure is dead while she liveth.
>
> 1 Timothy 5:6 KJV

Inside each of us is a war going on. There is a battle to the finish between the flesh and the spirit, and often, the spirit is willing but the flesh is weak. The flesh would give in to temptations, allow the pleasures, and cave to its desires if left to its own devices. It takes a wise Christian to realize that everything that feels good to this old flesh and every carnal thing that would make you smile in temporary delight is not spiritually edifying. In fact, it could be the equivalent of spiritual suicide. The blessed Word of God instructs us to walk after the spirit so that we won't mind the things of the flesh. When we are led by the spirit, the lusts of the flesh have no dominion over us.

The Bible lets us know that to be carnally minded is enmity against God (see Romans 8:6–7). We cannot please the Lord when we are following after our own lusts. And let's face it; we all have an area in our spiritual growth and development that we must guard diligently in order to keep our actions and desires "good for us." James 1:14–15 says, "But every man is tempted when he is drawn away of his own lust, and enticed. Then when lust hath conceived, it bringeth forth sin: and sin, when it is finished, bringeth forth death." Let us be led by the spirit that we might please the Lord.

It may feel very good to tell somebody off, give him a piece of your mind, but it's not good for the spirit. The Word of God asks, "Doth a fountain send forth at the same place sweet water and bitter?" (James 3:11 KJV). How can we speak blessings into the lives of others if we are speaking harsh words and curses? We seek not to please this flesh with the momentary gratification of an eye for an eye. No, we must follow Jesus's example of turning the other cheek and allow his grace to be sufficient.

It may also *feel good* to the flesh to engage in lustful thoughts and imaginations, to look upon someone, to lust after them, but Job said, "I made a covenant with mine eyes; why then should I think upon a maid?" (Job 31:1 KJV). The flesh may be pleased with such actions, but the spirit agonizes in sexual sin, even the contemplation of such. By the power of God's Spirit, we are overcomers, "[c]asting down imaginations, and every high thing that exalteth itself against the knowledge of God, and bringing into captivity every thought to the obedience of Christ" (2 Corinthians 10:5 KJV). Wow! Even our thoughts can be brought under subjection to the Lord. Wickedness of the mind does not have to be.

It may feel good to the flesh to engage in sinful acts, but the spirit mourns a slow death in our disobedience, for the Word of God states, "And she that liveth in pleasure is dead while she liveth" (1 Timothy 5:6 KJV). We must make a covenant with our hearts to think on things that are "true, honest, just, pure, lovely, and of a good report" (see Philippians 4:8 KJV). Wait a minute. Does that mean I can't enjoy life? Am I not allowed to have any fun or pleasure? Am I *dead* if I have a little fun? Of course not. The idea to embrace is that *sin is not entitled to our bodies* for Apostle Paul says that he "keep[s] under [his] body, and bring[s] it into subjection: lest that by any means, when [he has] preached to others, [he himself] should be a castaway" (1 Corinthians 9:27 KJV). How wonderful is the power and grace of God that it can keep us from falling!

Saints of God, don't be deceived. God's way is a way of joy and peace. When we yield to his Spirit, he will "fill [our] mouth[s] with laughter and [our] lips with shouts of joy" (Job 8:21 KJV). We know that "[i]n his presence is fullness of joy and at his right hand pleasures forevermore" (see Psalms 16:11 KJV). Just trust in him and the God of hope [will] fill you with all joy and peace as you do so, and you will find yourself overflowing with hope by the power of the Holy Spirit (see Romans 15:13 KJV).

Time to think about it

What is God revealing to me through today's devotion?

_____

_____

_____

_____

What is one specific thing I can do to apply this lesson to my life?

_____

_____

_____

DAY 39: BEWARE OF WOLVES IN SHEEP'S CLOTHING

> Beware of false prophets which come to you in sheep's clothing, but inwardly they are ravening wolves.
>
> Matthew 7:15 KJV

He speaks one thing, but his life doesn't become the gospel. He lives one thing before the public's eye, but behind the scene, his life is troubled. We have seen men become lifted in pride, only to utterly fall. For these reasons, the apostle Paul writes to Timothy that a bishop "must be blameless" (1 Timothy 3:2 KJV). He also states that he must not be "a novice, lest being lifted up with pride he fall into the condemnation of the devil" (v. 6 KJV). The true man of God is a gift from above, a leader of the flock, equipped with wisdom and a readiness to impart life to those who hear him. What a blessing he is!

In Matthew 7:16 KJV, Jesus talked about wolves in sheep clothing and good trees, which yield good fruit. He said, "Ye shall know them by their fruits." Jesus is the example. He says, "My sheep hear my voice, and I know them, and they follow me: And I give unto them eternal life; and they shall never perish, neither shall any man pluck them out of my hand" (John 10:27–28 KJV). Truth compels. Truth draws. Truth attracts. It is so important that we don't follow that which is false. It is so important to seek truth in God's word for Jesus declares, "Not every one that saith unto me, Lord, Lord, shall enter into the kingdom of heaven; but he that doeth the will of my Father which is in heaven" (Matthew 7:21 KJV).

Jesus goes on to say that "[m]any will say to me in that day, Lord, Lord, have we not prophesied in thy name? and in thy name have cast out devils? and in thy name done many wonderful works? And then will I profess unto them, I never knew you; depart from me, ye that work iniquity" (Matthew 7:22–23 KJV).

So how can one avoid the wolves? To be honest, it would require too much painstaking effort to identify all the counterfeits in the world. Instead, focus on the true! God's Word declares that a bishop be,

> [T]he husband of but one wife, temperate, self-controlled, respectable, hospitable, able to teach, not given to drunkenness, not violent but gentle, not quarrelsome, not a lover of money. He must manage his own family well and see that his children obey him with proper respect. (If anyone does not know how to manage his own family, how can he take care of God's church?) He must not be a recent convert, or he may become conceited and fall under the same judgment as the devil. He must also have

> a good reputation with outsiders, so that he will not fall into disgrace and into the devil's trap.
>
> 1 Timothy 3:2–7 NIV

That's a mighty tall order, but God expects his word to be kept. When a leader follows the heart of God, he is loved and respected among the flock. They give him honor for it is due him. He can stand before God and with joy, give an account of the souls of the saints entrusted to his care, for they will obey him as their leader and follow him as he follows Christ. This is the will of God, and it is beautiful.

Let us remember to praise God for godly leaders. Praise God for those of the cloth who hold up the blood-stained banner, standing in the gap for the saints, preaching and teaching the unadulterated Word of God. Let us praise God continually for those who admonish the people to amend their ways, to repent, and to follow God. Their feet are indeed beautiful (see Romans 10:15). Let us learn and follow after those leaders who stand in truth because those who are counterfeits will ultimately bring destruction. The Word says, "For the leaders of this people cause them to err; and they that are led of them are destroyed" (Isaiah 9:16 KJV). Jesus said in Matthew 15:14, "Every plant, which my heavenly Father hath not planted, shall be rooted up. Let them alone: they be blind leaders of the blind. And if the blind lead the blind, both shall fall into the ditch" (KJV). Beware of the wolves in sheep's clothing. Beware!

Time to think about it

What is God revealing to me through today's devotion?

_____

_____

_____

_____

What is one specific thing I can do to apply this lesson to my life?

_____

_____

_____

_____

DAY 40: FOOLS RUSH IN WHERE [WISE MEN] FEAR TO TREAD

> Go not forth hastily to strive, lest thou know not what to do in the end thereof, when thy neighbor hath put thee to shame.
>
> Proverbs 25:8 KJV

In the twenty plus years that I've been walking with God, I have found that serving God takes wisdom and obedience to his Holy Word. Walking in the way of the Lord requires cautious steps and watchful eyes. Jesus said, "Take heed that ye be not deceived: for many shall come in my name, saying, I am Christ: and the time draweth near; go ye not therefore after them" (Luke 21:8 KJV). Precious hearts of God, don't rush to be deceived but take heed the signs of the time.

In the scripture referenced above, we see that over two thousand years ago, the disciples wanted to know what signs would indicate the end times. Today, we still ask the question "when will the end be?" This is an age old question, and I believe that saints and sinners alike desire to know the answer. Well, one thing is for certain: the time is drawing closer and closer. Yes, as Andre Crouch wrote in his timeless song, "Soon and very soon we are going to see the king," for Jesus is coming back to meet us in the air. The signs are here. They are all around us, and we can't ignore them. Sometimes, I wish that I had a huge neon sign to hang at the church's exit, reminding us, "Warning: Danger is ahead!" "Warning: Proceed with caution!" or "Warning: Enter this world at your own risk!"

Sadly, many people don't believe in the fast-approaching return of Jesus Christ, and they rush about in places of danger where those with wisdom fear to go. They take no thought for their eternal souls and fail to make preparations, but the Bible warns us to be ready as the time approaches. Luke 12:40 says, "Son of man cometh at an hour when ye think not" (KJV). No one knows the moment of Jesus's return, but it is a smart move to be prepared.

Sometimes, while traveling along highways, I can't help but notice a lot of road signs along the way—some bright yellow, some green with glow-in-the-dark white lettering, some red, some black and white, some flashing, and some with reflectors. What I find really interesting is the simplicity of theses signs. Road signs, like the Word of God, are simple. When one is in danger, is there really time to read through a lot of words? No, the message needs to be quick and clear. My granddaddy used to say that the Word of God is written so that a fool won't err and a blind man won't miss the way. In other words, one can't be lost when he's walking in the Word of God. Think about it. These road signs read simple messages, such as Stop, Wrong Way, Yield, No U-turn, Dead End, and No Outlet.

In the Word, Jesus also kept his warnings simple: Take heed, Watch, or Beware "that ye be not deceived." When men come saying that they are Christ, follow the advice on the stop sign and stop. Don't tread after them. When you hear of wars and rumors of wars, the Bible says don't be afraid for these things must come. Follow the caution sign for it alerts you that if you're saved, stay saved. If not, get saved.

The green light has changed to yellow and we must, like many would say, "clear the intersection." Get out of the way of unrighteousness, sin, death and destruction, and hell's fire. In wisdom, seek safety. Yield to the holiness of Christ Jesus. Romans 6:16 says, "Know ye not, that to whom ye yield yourselves servants to obey, his servants ye are to whom ye obey; whether of sin unto death, or of obedience unto righteousness?" (KJV) Yield yourselves to God. Submit to him, and he will do the rest.

Romans 6:12–13 says, "Let not sin therefore reign in your mortal body, that ye should obey it in the lusts thereof. Neither yield ye your members as instruments of unrighteousness unto sin: but yield yourselves unto God, as those that are alive from the dead, and your members as instruments of righteousness unto God" (KJV).

Don't rush into traps and snares laid by the enemy, avoid evil, and dodge the allure of unrighteousness. Allow wisdom to lead you cautiously home. If you find yourself on a dead-end street, retrace your steps and study the signs. God allows U-turns. Turn around and repent, for the kingdom of God is closer than you think. "Watch ye, therefore, and pray always, that ye may be accounted worthy to escape all the things that shall come to pass, and to stand before the Son of man" (Luke 21:36 KJV). Don't be a fool—rushing in where those who are wise are afraid to go.

Time to think about it

What is God revealing to me through today's devotion?

_____

_____

_____

_____

What is one specific thing I can do to apply this lesson to my life?

_____

_____

_____

_____

DAY 41: TO ERR IS HUMAN, TO FORGIVE DIVINE

> For if ye forgive men their trespasses, your heavenly Father will also forgive you.
>
> Matthew 6:14 KJV

We are all human, imperfect beings, and as such, we are prone to make mistakes. Sometimes, our errors are the result of poor choices, often deliberate and intentional, even apathetic and selfish. Jeremiah 17:9 says, "The heart is deceitful above all things, and desperately wicked: who can know it?" (KJV) What horrible things we are sometimes capable of doing! Yet, the heart that is capable of forgiving such acts is a heart that is truly God-touched—*divine*. We've all read (or heard) the scripture, "Forgive, and ye shall be forgiven" (Luke 6:37 KJV). Still, the road to forgiveness, especially the forgiveness of oneself, is often rough and winding.

When I was seventeen years old, about to graduate from high school, the one thing I wanted most in the world was a car. I would be leaving for college in a few months, and having my own transportation was the beginning and ending of all my thoughts. So I turned to the one person I knew who could and would help me—my granddaddy, Daddy Johnnie.

When I approached him, he told me he'd have to think about it and would get back to me. When he finally did, he told me that another relative also had come to him, needing money. She was a single mother with five children and desperately needed help to provide for her family. Obviously, her situation was direr than mine, yet Daddy Johnnie told me that the decision was mine to make. I had to choose. I could get a car and ignore the needs of others, or I could allow Daddy Johnnie to help them, and he would give me the money for a new wardrobe for college. I'd like to tell you that I chose the latter and that everyone lived happily ever after. On the contrary, the selfish seventeen-year-old chose the car, and yes, the female relative and her children lost their home.

That decision plagued me for years. I tried to blame my granddaddy for even placing such a major decision in the hands of one so young, but ultimately I had to accept responsibility for what I caused. After many years, I finally called this relative to say that I was sorry. The funny thing is she never blamed me and didn't even know that I was involved. Her forgiveness came easily, and I was grateful for it. However, my forgiving myself took a lot more effort. I finally did but only with the help of God.

Sometimes we fail at life's little tests. We make the wrong decision and commit acts that are motivated by selfishness or spite. Ultimately, we must make amends and seek forgiveness for those actions, realizing that our Father in heaven forgives us the moment we ask him to and that he also provides enough grace in the situation so that we may also forgive one another as well as ourselves, and eventually we learn the lesson: "To err is human, to forgive divine" (Alexander Pope, "An Essay on Criticism").

Time to think about it

What is God revealing to me through today's devotion?

___

___

___

___

What is one specific thing I can do to apply this lesson to my life?

___

___

___

___

DAY 42: YOU CAN'T PULL THE WOOL OVER MY EYES

> And Jesus answered and said unto them, Take heed that no man deceive you.
>
> Matthew 24:4 KJV

Ma Dear was a master at detecting dishonesty. She told us—Ronnie, Karen, B.B. and me—over and over again that we couldn't *pull the wool over her eyes*. In fact, she told us that while we were *trying to*, she was knitting it and throwing it back over our eyes. She said this so much that we didn't dare try to fool her. We feared that she had this supernatural ability to peer into our minds and know every mischievous plot, every deceptive plan—everything—like who broke the gravy bowl to her favorite china set, who tracked mud into the house and didn't clean it up, who left the bathroom light on, or who spilled the red Kool-Aid on her white lace tablecloth. Ma Dear also had a special look—her head lowered, eyebrows raised, mouth twisted, and eyes gazing upwardly—that clearly spoke, "You're not fooling me!" Was she a wise woman? Absolutely. Was it discernment? Perhaps. Whatever it was, we didn't play around with Ma Dear.

Such fear of what we thought was Ma Dear's Louisiana-bred, supernatural ability reminds me a lot of the awe and reverence we, as children of God, must have for his all-seeing eye. Would we dare to fool our God? I think not. We couldn't if we tried for he sees all and knows all. He is omniscient and omnipresent. He is the source of all wisdom and knowledge. Proverbs 2:6 says, "For the LORD giveth wisdom: out of his mouth cometh knowledge and understanding" (KJV). It is futile to think we can *get one over* on God.

Likewise, made in the image of God, *we* are not to be deceived by man, especially concerning the coming of the Lord. Jesus said, "For many shall come in my name, saying, I am Christ; and shall deceive many" (Matthew 24:5). He goes on to list the many horrors to follow, with the love of many waxing cold (Matthew 24:12 KJV). Brothers and sisters, the Lord has not left us ignorant. He has told us what to watch for and said, "Therefore be ye also ready for in such an hour as ye think not the Son of man cometh" (verse 44 KJV). If any of us lack wisdom, we only need to ask God, and he will give it to us freely and abundantly (see James 1:5 KJV) that we may not be deceived by the tempter. What good news to hear: "Happy is the man that findeth wisdom, and the man that getteth understanding" (Proverbs 3:13 KJV).

So, we can't pull the wool over God's eyes, and as children of God, he won't allow the wool to be pulled over our eyes. Let us walk in wisdom for the Word of

God declares, "Wisdom is the principal thing; *therefore* get wisdom: and with all thy getting get understanding" (Proverbs 4:7 KJV).

Time to think about it

What is God revealing to me through today's devotion?

_____

_____

_____

_____

What is one specific thing I can do to apply this lesson to my life?

_____

_____

_____

_____

DAY 43: FOOL ME ONCE, SHAME ON YOU; FOOL ME TWICE, SHAME ON ME

> Yet if any man suffer as a Christian, let him not be ashamed; but let him glorify God on this behalf.
>
> 1 Peter 4:16 KJV

"How could I have been so stupid?" This is the question we ask ourselves when we find that we have fallen victim to deception, again. There have been many times in my life when I have felt gullible and naive. Those were times when I allowed a friend or loved one to disappoint me or take advantage of me one too many times. Honestly, it belittles and makes a person feel bad. Nevertheless, the truth of the matter is that if I had it to do over again, I would probably render myself just as before and be fooled again. Some might say I'm a glutton for pain, a fool, and even call me stupid, but I don't see it quite like that. I'm not responsible for how people treat me. I'm only responsible for how I respond to their treatment and how I ultimately treat them. The only time we should feel ashamed of our behavior is when *we* ourselves behave ungodly, not when we suffer for the sake of righteousness.

So what should we do when someone has mistreated or deceived us more than once? Do we cut that person off, never to trust them again? Do we place a steel door between them and our hearts to keep them out? Do we handle them with a long-handled spoon? The answer to all of these questions is *no*. It is never okay, never biblical, never Christ-like to stop loving someone. In 1 John 3:17, the writer asks, "But whoso hath this world's good, and seeth his brother have need, and shut up his bowels of compassion from him, how dwelleth the love of God in him?" (KJV) If this verse applies to mammon, then how much more should this Word direct us in extending love, hope, mercy, and grace? There is no limit to the number of times we are to extend a helping hand or offer words of life to an individual. Of course, we try to establish such limits, but where does God okay them? Do good continually and watch the world wonder. In 1 Corinthians 4:9b–10, Paul gives the apostolic example of humility and patience, stating that the apostles "are made a spectacle unto the world, and to angels, and to men. We are fools for Christ's sake, but ye are wise in Christ; we are weak, but ye are strong; ye are honorable, but we despised" (KJV). The world will not understand us. They will not grasp how "being reviled, we bless; being persecuted, we suffer it: [and] Being defamed, we intreat" (verses 12–13 KJV).

As servants of the Lord, we wear the garments of praise, adorned with humility and patience. Longsuffering and gentleness are our shoes, enabling us to stand and say, "Fool me once, shame on you; but, fool me twice, to God be the glory!"

Time to think about it

What is God revealing to me through today's devotion?

_____

_____

_____

_____

What is one specific thing I can do to apply this lesson to my life?

_____

_____

_____

_____

DAY 44: GOD GAVE ME TWO EARS AND ONLY ONE MOUTH SO I CAN LISTEN TWICE AS MUCH AS I SPEAK

> Wherefore, my beloved brethren, let every man be swift to hear, slow to speak, slow to wrath.
>
> James 1:19 KJV

The Bible tells us to study to be quiet (1 Thessalonians 4:11 KJV), and it is with good reason. The tongue is a little member that boasts great things (James 3:5 KJV). It is compared to the bridle that is used to control the entire body of the horse and the small helm that is used to maneuver the greatest ship. Yes, our tongue is unruly, and no man can tame it (James 3:8 KJV). We think it, and we have to say it. If it comes up, it must come out. This ought not to be. James also writes, "If any man offend not in word, the same is a perfect man and able also to bridle the whole body" (James 3:2 KJV). When a man bridles his tongue, he has indeed mastered himself.

I am reminded of a story I read in a literature book once:

Learning to Be Silent

> The pupils of the Tendai school used to study meditation before Zen entered Japan. Four of them who were intimate friends promised one another to observe seven days of silence.
>
> On the first day all were silent. Their meditation had begun auspiciously, but when night came and the oil lamps were growing dim, one of the pupils could not help exclaiming to a servant: "Fix those lamps."
>
> The second pupil was surprised to hear the first one talk: "We are not supposed to say a word," he remarked.
>
> "You two are stupid. Why did you talk?" asked the third.
>
> "I am the only one who has not talked," concluded the fourth pupil.
>
> (Diyanni, Literature—
Reading Fiction, Poetry and Drama)

Although it seems comical, this story clearly illustrates man's inability to keep silent, his need to communicate, and maybe a little bit of pride. As children of God, we must grow in God's grace, and that involves learning to listen. It is God's will. One thing we know for sure is that "[f]aith cometh by hearing," (Romans 10:17 KJV) and not by speaking. We can't *talk* our way into faith, but we can surely *hear* our way there, and it is no accident. The fact that God gave us two ears and one mouth just might serve as a tiny reminder of his will and expectation.

Time to think about it

What is God revealing to me through today's devotion?

_____

_____

_____

_____

What is one specific thing I can do to apply this lesson to my life?

_____

_____

_____

_____

DAY 45: EVERYTHING THAT COMES UP DOESN'T HAVE TO COME OUT

> He that keepeth his mouth keepeth his life: but he that openeth wide his lips shall have destruction.
>
> Proverbs 13:3 KJV

There is great power in the tongue! In Mark 11:23, Jesus said, "For verily I say unto you, That whosoever shall say unto this mountain, Be thou removed, and be thou cast into the sea; and shall not doubt in his heart, but shall believe that those things which he saith shall come to pass; he shall have whatsoever he saith" (KJV). When we apply our belief to our spoken words, we activate a power that is greater than ourselves. Because of this, we can also sometimes find ourselves *hung by the tongue*. We must learn to watch our mouths, for inside of them are little members that can kindle a great fire. But how do we accomplish this?

In living for God, there is a chain of command on the inside of us. We have a spirit that must be regenerated by the Holy Spirit, for God communicates with us through our spirit man. Then we have the heart or mind of man that must be conformed to God's Word and led by the Spirit. Thirdly, we have a physical body that must be offered as a living sacrifice to carry out what is in the heart of man. It is extremely important as Christians that we submit wholeheartedly to God so that our whole being is aligned with the Spirit of God. This is the key to walking in obedience and righteousness concerning our lips.

However, aligning ourselves with the Lord is not about religion and vain actions. This submission is centered upon a powerful, life-changing relationship with Jesus. James 1:26 says, "If any man among you seem to be religious, and bridleth not his tongue, but deceiveth his own heart, that man's religion is vain" (KJV). It is especially needful that we close our mouths when what we have to say will do more harm than good. Sometimes, we claim that things just "hop out." This should not be, for our words are an extension of ourselves and reveal who we are on the inside. Children of God are builders, not burners. When things just "hop out" of our mouths, consider the following:

- Whoso privily slandereth his neighbor, him will I cut off (Psalm 101:5 KJV).
- Let no corrupt communication proceed out of your mouth, but that which is good to the use of edifying that it may minister grace to the hearers (Ephesians 4:29 KJV).
- Suffer not thy mouth to cause thy flesh to sin; neither say thou before the angel, that it was

> an error: wherefore should God be angry at thy voice, and destroy the work of thine hands? (Ecclesiastes 5:6 KJV)

We must not be guilty of "I said that, but I didn't mean it" or "I'm sorry. I didn't mean to hurt your feelings." Out of your heart, your mouth speaks (see Luke 6:45 KJV), and it has the ability to crush and contaminate. Once uttered, those hurtful words cannot be taken back. Let us apply the word of God to our lips that we might know God's truths. Proverbs 16:23–24 says, "The heart of the wise teacheth his mouth, and added learning to his lips. Pleasant words are as a honeycomb, sweet to the soul, and health to the bones" (KJV). Stay in the Word; follow the chain of command. Everything that comes up doesn't have to come out. Let the Spirit filter.

Time to think about it

What is God revealing to me through today's devotion?

_____

_____

_____

_____

What is one specific thing I can do to apply this lesson to my life?

_____

_____

_____

_____

DAY 46: DON'T CUT OFF YOUR NOSE TO SPITE YOUR FACE

> Recompense to no man evil for evil. Provide things honest in the sight of all men. If it be possible, as much as lieth in you, live peaceably with all men. Dearly beloved, avenge not yourselves, but rather give place unto wrath: for it is written, Vengeance is mine; I will repay, saith the Lord.
>
> Romans 12:17–19 KJV

Revenge is always a self-destructive act. Even if our seeking revenge provides a sense of satisfaction, it is usually short lived and soon turns to guilt. Additionally, one's honor, dignity, self-respect, and peace are sacrificed by him who takes matters of vengeance in his own hands. The consequence of disobeying God is far too great for the momentary satisfaction of acting out one's wrath. When we are offended by someone, our obligation to that person and to ourselves is to go to that person and immediately set things in order.

An eye for an eye is not applicable in the Christian heart, but forgiveness is the New Testament order and only option.

Paul writes in Romans 12:20–21, "Therefore if thine enemy hunger, feed him: if he thirst, give him drink… Be not overcome of evil, but overcome evil with good" (KJV). To shut up our bowels of compassion toward anyone, particularly if we are "getting even" with them, is like cutting off our noses to spite our faces. We end up hurting ourselves and losing just as much as the person whom we are trying to hurt. Our soul suffers because our behavior is unbecoming the gospel that we have been commissioned to live. Think about it: We receive little to no spiritual edification for doing *good* to those who are good to us. Oh, but when we exercise goodness toward those who hurt us, those who talk about us, those who have wounded us in some way, or those who clearly do not like us, *then* we show forth the love of Christ, and we honor the perfect example of his life, his love, and his grace.

We have to be very careful and diligent about quickly releasing those hard feelings that come our way. They only serve to calcify our love for one another and harden our hearts. Who is left hurt? Usually we are. When tests and trials come against us, they come to make us strong, yet we sometimes give them the power to stifle us, strangle us, and make us weak. Let's not behave in disobedience and rebellion when we face difficult times because when we do, we really do suffer, and we cause those around us to suffer as well.

Time to think about it

What is God revealing to me through today's devotion?

_____

_____

_____

_____

What is one specific thing I can do to apply this lesson to my life?

_____

_____

_____

_____

DAY 47: GOD DOESN'T LIKE UGLY, AND HE'S NOT STUCK ON PRETTY!

> When a man's ways please the LORD, he maketh even his enemies to be at peace with him.
>
> Proverbs 16:7 KJV

I wish I had a dollar for every time I heard Ma Dear say, "She's a pretty girl, but she has some ugly ways." I would probably have enough money for a mini-vacation. Since God is not concerned with our outward cuteness, we can safely conclude that he sees straight past the outer beauty to the inner beauty. The only ugliness we can ever possess *in his eyes* is the ugliness of unrighteousness and sin. Our ways and attitudes reveal the true state of our hearts, and we must strive at all times to make sure our ways please the Lord.

If we take a good look through the Word of God and thoroughly examine ourselves, we just might find that there are some characteristics lurking about inside us that are just not pleasing to the Lord. Proverbs 6:16–19 tells us of the seven things that God hates: a proud look, a lying tongue, hands that shed innocent blood, a heart that devises wicked imaginations, feet that are swift in running to mischief, a false witness that speaketh lies, and he that sows discord among the brethren (KJV). Such ugliness displeases the Father. There can be no debate over what's ugly when measured against the Word of God and what he finds pleasing or displeasing, for the Word of God is clear and true.

It is important to note that our own righteousness does not make us pleasing in the eyes of God. It is his righteousness that makes us beautiful. The Scriptures declare, "The Lord taketh pleasure in his people: he will beautify the meek with salvation" (Psalms 149:4 KJV). Salvation is beautiful, and when we come to know the Lord as our savior, his beauty rests in us and upon us. Again, it's not about our righteousness because our righteousness is "as filthy rags" (Isaiah 64:6). We must be clothed in the righteousness and humility of the Lord. Even then, we have no cause to boast for the Word also says that the righteous are scarcely going to make it into God's kingdom. In other words, even at our best, we cannot impress the holiness of God. It is only in radiating his presence in our lives that we please him. The Lord is moved by our faith in him—living a life before him that seeks to bring him glory. Then, and only then, are our ways pleasing to our God.

Time to think about it

What is God revealing to me through today's devotion?

_____

_____

_____

_____

What is one specific thing I can do to apply this lesson to my life?

_____

_____

_____

_____

DAY 48:
TELL ONE LIE AND YOU'LL HAVE TO TELL TWO

> Wherefore putting away lying, speak every man truth with his neighbor: for we are members one of another.
>
> Ephesians 4:25 KJV

Our voices chimed throughout the neighborhood, and the claps and pats of our little hands beat the rhythm for our words,

> Miss Suzy had a steamboat
> The steamboat had a bell
> Miss Suzy went to heaven
> The steamboat went to-
> Hello operator!
> Give me number nine.
> If you disconnect me,
> I'll kick your big be-
> 'Hind the 'frigerator,
> There was a piece of glass.
> Miss Suzy fell upon it
> And cut her big old-

> Ask me no more questions,
> I'll tell you no lies!

I hear our voices as plainly now as I did then, warning the hearers that if they didn't want to be told any more lies, then they should avoid asking questions. Have you ever felt like that in dealing with someone? Sir Walter Scott wrote, "Oh what a tangled web we weave, / When first we practice to deceive!" (*Marmion*, 6.17). How right he was. One lie only leads to another. Once that first lie is told, it sets off a domino effect, and another lie must be told to either cover up or facilitate the first lie. It becomes a vicious cycle of deception and dishonesty, one that cannot be easily escaped.

In "One lie leads to another lie," Francis Duggan writes in the second stanza:

> One lie leads to another lie that always is the case
> Your first lie for deception and your second to save face
> And when you are faced with the truth, the truth you will deny
> And to lie to you comes easy, so you tell another lie.

That is the gist of it. Lying is habit forming. We've all met that person who seemingly lies unnecessarily. "Why?" we ask. The lies just seem so pointless. It is sad that so many people fear the scorn, rejection, or disapproval of others to the point of ignoring their fear for God. That is, after all, what it boils down to. When we lie to save face, protect feelings, or protect our own image, we are essentially admitting that we fear man and his reaction more than we fear God and the consequences of the sin of lying. Nevertheless, the Bible is clear: "But the fearful, and unbelieving, and the abominable, and murderers, and whoremongers, and sorcerers, and idolaters, and all liars, shall have their part in the lake which burneth with fire and brimstone: which is the second death" (Revelation 21:8 KJV). The liar, whose sin to us may seem lesser than the others mentioned, is nonetheless grouped with sinners whose iniquities carry the wages of death. Don't be deceived! This shows the importance of honesty in the sight of God. Saints, let us strive to please God, to fear him only and serve him with integrity.

Time to think about it

What is God revealing to me through today's devotion?

_____

_____

_____

_____

What is one specific thing I can do to apply this lesson to my life?

_____

_____

_____

_____

DAY 49: A WHISTLING WOMAN AND A CACKLING HEN ALWAYS COME TO NO GOOD END

> But let it be the hidden man of the heart, in that which is not corruptible, even the ornament of a meek and quiet spirit, which is in the sight of God of great price.
>
> 1 Peter 3:4

I first heard this expression from my great granddaddy, Daddy Buster. Daddy Buster was the most gentle-hearted man I have ever known, and I remember him fondly. A retired mechanic, he came to live with Ma Dear and us after suffering a stroke that left him with right-sided weakness. He was around eighty years old at the time and was an insulin-dependent diabetic. Spending time with Daddy Buster can only be described as a treat. Because he was so kind and appreciative of every little thing a person did for him, one didn't mind doing all he/she could: preparing his meals, giving him his daily insulin injections, even spending hours of precious teenage years reading to him or talking with him. He always knew what to say! Take for example the day I set my mind on learning how to whistle, I was growing more and more frustrated with my repeated failure, but my great granddaddy was there to assuage my frustration.

Daddy Buster and I were sitting on the front porch of Ma Dear's house, enjoying the evening breeze and the smell of freshly cut grass that wafted by with every stir of the wind. I was fifteen years old at the time and bent on mastering the skill of whistling. Until then, I had only been able to generate a sound remotely close to the whistle by sucking air *into* my mouth through tightly puckered lips. Desperately, I wanted to whistle the *right way*, blowing the air out! Daddy Buster sat and watched me for a while before finally saying, "Baby, let me tell you something. Don't worry about whistling. That's nothing you wanna do anyways 'cause a whistling woman and a cackling hen, they always come to no good end." I sat for a moment, allowing his words their opportunity to convince me of what Daddy Buster was saying. I admit that I didn't see the relevance at all and didn't understand it one bit. The only thing I could see at the time was that I wasn't doing *something* right because the sound coming from my lips was the sound of smooth wind, signifying nothing, and not the sharp, screeching sound I was hoping for, the one that sounds like the alarm of a tea kettle. I wasn't happy, and his words didn't help much.

Since that time, of course, I have learned to whistle by blowing the air out; in fact, I can no longer whistle by drawing in. I've also had a lot of time to think about Daddy Buster's words, and I think I've found the significance in what he was saying. Maybe he was trying to encourage me to see that the whistling woman and the crowing hen are not only sources of unnecessary noise, and perhaps even annoying noise to some, but they are perhaps unbecoming. The rooster crows, not the hen, so she is out of nature's order. Some, and perhaps the person who coined this expression, feels that the woman also displays masculine behavior by whistling. I can't say that I agree, but that's the best I can come up with. Both are drawing attention to themselves through actions considered unnatural to them. Instead, women are expected to adorn a meek and quiet spirit. I still like to whistle a happy tune from time to time, so forgive me, Daddy Buster. I hope you don't mind.

Time to think about it

What is God revealing to me through today's devotion?

_____

_____

_____

_____

What is one specific thing I can do to apply this lesson to my life?

_____

_____

_____

_____

DAY 50: THINK BEFORE YOU SPEAK

> He that answereth a matter before he heareth it, it is folly and shame unto him.
>
> Proverbs 18:13 KJV

No matter how we'd like to believe we can take back the words we speak, once a word is uttered, it cannot be erased. If it hurts or destroys, healing is possible, but pain still received a temporary home. Ecclesiastes 5:2 says, "Be not rash with thy mouth, and let not thine heart be hasty to utter anything before God: for God is in heaven, and thou upon earth: therefore let thy words be few" (KJV).

It is always right to think before we speak, *always*, but the truth of the matter is stinking thinking can lead to reeking speaking. Therefore, even our thinking and self-talk must be guarded. "It is not that which goeth into the mouth that defiles a man, but it is that which comes out of the mouth" (Matthew 15:11 KJV). We can make sure that our utterances are clean by making sure they are first filtered through a transformed mind. The Greek word for transformed is *metamorphosis*. When a caterpillar is morphed from a worm into a butterfly, he is never to return to his former state for he has been transformed. When the heart and mind are changed, the mouth is changed, and that old way of thinking, speaking, and being must be denied reentry.

In Matthew 12:34 – 37 Jesus says,

> O generation of vipers, how can ye, being evil, speak good things? For out of the abundance of the heart the mouth speaketh. A good man out of the good treasure of the heart bringeth forth good things: and an evil man out of the evil treasure bringeth forth evil things. But I say unto you, That every idle word that men shall speak, they shall give account thereof in the day of judgment. For by thy words thou shalt be justified, and by thy words thou shalt be condemned (KJV).

The tongue will hang us if we aren't diligent about yielding it to Jesus. This applies even to what we say to ourselves: "I'm not lovable," "I'll never get out of debt," "I've always had a quick temper," or "I speak my mind! That's just the way I am." These thoughts come to us, and we must think before we utter them.

Also, let us be kind to others with our words and minister grace, for people are drawn to those who affirm them and are repelled by those who are always critical. Think and then speak health, wealth, freedom, safety, spiritual growth, and prosperity. Confess life; confess the promises of God! Say like the psalmist in Psalms 17:3, "Thou hast proven my heart; thou hast visited me in the night; thou hast tried me, and shall find nothing; I am purposed that my mouth shall not transgress."

We overcome by the blood of Jesus and the words of our testimony. It's a promise and a done deal! Testify these things:

- I am saved by his blood.
- I am healed by his stripes.
- I am delivered by his plan.
- I am free in Christ Jesus.
- I have all things according to his riches.
- I can do all things by his power.
- I am blessed in the city.
- I am blessed in the field.
- I am blessed when I come and when I go.

Think before you speak so that *good* words might be manifested as truth.

Time to think about it

What is God revealing to me through today's devotion?

_____

_____

_____

_____

What is one specific thing I can do to apply this lesson to my life?

_____

_____

_____

_____

DAY 51: SLOW AND STEADY WINS THE RACE

> I returned, and saw under the sun, that the race is not to the swift, nor the battle to the strong.
>
> Ecclesiastes 9:11 KJV

Slow and steady wins the race. I've seen this in love, in church, in school, in most areas of life. People who take off fueled by zeal and excitement but with little commitment and perseverance often run out of gas along the way. It is the committed individual, the one who decides from the start that he or she is going to see the race to the end, who makes it across the finish line.

One of the most valuable lessons a person can learn in serving the Lord is to take life one day at a time, focusing on pleasing God with growth and spiritual maturity that develops over time. Often, the overzealous Christian runs out of gas after lap one, the first test, the initiating trial, that gargantuan trial that swallows them whole as in the case of Steve and Veronica.

When I first came to the Lord, he placed me in the company of two beautiful people, a young couple, Steve and Veronica. We joined church around the same time and were really close. We enjoyed many dinners in our home or theirs, and we traveled to Sunday morning worship together. The first two years of my saved life, my husband was not attending church with me, so I was Steve and Veronica's tagalong. We often discussed the Word of God and shared testimonies en route to service, and they blessed me. I remember the excitement these two continually showed for serving God. They exhibited such a zeal and unquenchable enthusiasm for the lord that I loved being with them! Thus, the beauty of their being a couple in Christ and worshipping together inspired me. I remember Steve sang louder than anyone in the church and often off-key. Their devotion to the things of God led them to be in attendance every time the church doors opened.

Steve would sit in service and take pleasure in teasing me every time a line or phrase uttered by the preacher would *hit me* or hit my home. I, on the other hand, usually sat in service afraid that I was not going to be able to actually live for this awesome and amazing God who loved me so much. How could I ever live up to being the person he expected me to be according to his Word when I felt that I was such a rotten mess? Other times, I sat in service fuming over Steve's teasing, while he smiled and laughed. It was a rough beginning, and things only slowly got better as I stayed put and learned of Christ. Jesus says in Matthew 11:29–30, "Take my yoke upon you, and learn of me; for I am meek and lowly in heart: and ye shall find rest unto your souls. For my yoke is easy, and my burden is light" (KJV). When we take the time to sit and learn of Jesus, our lives become settled in him, and he will keep us.

Today, I don't get the opportunity to see Steve or Veronica anymore. We have all moved to different parts of the country, and our communication with one another is next to nil. Veronica still serves the Lord with her whole heart and lives her life as a part of the body. However, she and Steve divorced years ago and have remarried other people. That zeal with which Steve began this race died out, and he's now on the sidelines, looking for a moment to jump back in. It is not always the one who starts out with the most speed who actually wins the race but the one who stands still and sticks around to see the salvation of the Lord.

Time to think about it

What is God revealing to me through today's devotion?

_____

_____

_____

_____

What is one specific thing I can do to apply this lesson to my life?

_____

_____

_____

_____

DAY 52: THE HAND THAT ROCKS THE CRADLE RULES THE WORLD

> She looketh well to the ways of her household, and eateth not the bread of idleness. Her children arise up, and call her blessed.
>
> Proverbs 31:27–28 KJV

In *Children's Rights and Others: A Book of Nursery Logic* (1892), Kate Douglas Wiggins writes, "Give me the first six years of a child's life, and I care not who has the rest." This profound statement indicates the importance of those first and most impressionable years of childhood, years when *mom* is usually the single most influential person in a child's world. William Ross Wallace wrote, "The hand that rocks the cradle rules the world," (1865) and there seems to be a lot of truth to the statement. The hand that rocks the cradle is the one that, *in the very least*, rules the house because those hands establish routine and create safety, love, and trust for children. They shape the person that the child is likely to become. That is why the Bible has much to say about rearing children.

Ephesians 6:4 instructs, "And ye, fathers, provoke not your children to wrath: but bring them up in the nurture and admonition of the Lord," (KJV). Teaching our children to fear God (see Deuteronomy 31:13 KJV), to be obedient to him, and to keep his word is of utmost importance. When we train our children in the way they should go, the Bible promises that they will not depart from it (see Proverbs 22:6 KJV). Sometimes, it may *seem* like they have gone astray as they venture into the world to discover it for themselves and make their own footprints in the sand, but we have an assurance that what has been planted in them has surely taken root and will one day bring forth fruit.

I'm inspired by my husband's testimony concerning this God-given certainty. When he was a child, growing up in Natchez, Mississippi, his parents had him in church more often than he cared to be. Weekly, he attended Sunday school, Sunday morning worship, Sunday evening worship, Monday night prayer, Tuesday night Bible study, Friday night evangelistic service, and Saturday evening young people's service. He spent much of his life in church with his parents. Once he graduated from high school and went off to college, he ventured off into the world, being led astray by his discovery of worldly pleasures and youthful lusts. However, what he had learned from being under the teaching of God's Word all of his life could not be taken away from him because it was rooted in his heart. He danced with the devil, but ultimately, he chose Jesus for a lifetime commitment. The enemy couldn't keep him because he had been given to God long before.

Sometimes it seems as if our children don't hear us or are not interested in hearing about God, but they are more receptive than we realize. When they are trained in the way, brought up in the fear and admonition of the Lord, the Lord will keep a rein on them, and when the time comes, he will draw them in. That's word, and that's our hope.

Time to think about it

What is God revealing to me through today's devotion?

_____

_____

_____

_____

What is one specific thing I can do to apply this lesson to my life?

_____

_____

_____

_____

DAY 53:
AN IDLE MIND IS THE DEVIL'S WORKSHOP

> Finally, brethren, whatsoever things are true, whatsoever things are honest, whatsoever things are just, whatsoever things are pure, whatsoever things are lovely, whatsoever things are of good report, if there be any virtue, and if there be any praise, think on these things.
>
> Philippians 4:8 KJV

Ralph Waldo Emerson once stated, "Beware of what you set your mind on for that you will surely become." If your thoughts are evil and left uncontrolled, not brought under the influence of Christ, your words, actions, and character ultimately becomes the product of those impure thoughts, in other words, evil. That is why it is important to meditate on the things the Bible has instructed us to think on, those things that are true, honest, just, pure, lovely, and of a good report. In doing so, these thoughts will manifest the same attributes in our character. Our mind and our thoughts must be governed by God.

The United Negro College Fund has a saying: "A mind is a terrible thing to waste." As Christians, we must strive to "exercise [ourselves]—our minds—unto godliness" (1 Timothy 4:7b KJV), "For bodily exercise profiteth little; but godliness is profitable unto all things, having promise of life that is now, and of that which is to come" (1 Timothy 4:8 KJV). When the mind is left idle, it becomes susceptible to trash and debris like a wasteland and dumping ground for the devil. It becomes his workshop. Yikes! Rest assured, my friend, your mind will be filled, but with what is up to you. Don't waste your thoughts on vain imaginations and things that do not edify. Instead, put a No Dumping sign on your thoughts and tell the enemy, "I choose to let the mind that is in me be like the mind that was in Christ Jesus" (see Philippians 2:5 KJV).

Still, this is the challenge of many—dying out to self—so we let *self* control our thoughts. We become fixed on the things of this world: the lust of the flesh, the lust of the eyes, and the pride of life. Are your thoughts motivated by the flesh, sensual desires, pride, or even inhibitions? Are your thoughts controlled by your eyes, what and how things appear to be? Remember, man looks on the outward appearance, but God looks on the heart. Consider the apostle Paul who wrote,

> And I, brethren, when I came to you, came not with excellency of speech or of wisdom, declaring unto you the testimony of God, For I determined not to know any thing among you, save Jesus Christ, and him crucified. And I was with you in weakness, and in fear, and

> in much trembling. And my speech and my preaching was not with enticing words of man's wisdom, but in demonstration of the Spirit and of power: That your faith should not stand in the wisdom of men, but in the power of God. (1 Corinthians 2:1–5 KJV)

Don't let your thoughts be consumed with impressing man with your beauty, intelligence, wealth or prosperity, fine clothes, or fine speech. Don't let your thoughts be consumed by the pride of this life. Galatians 6:3 says, "For if a man think himself to be something, when he is nothing, he [deceives] himself" (KJV).

Finally, we must realize that we are the handler of our thoughts. When they appear, we decide what to do with them. Second Corinthians 10:5 says, "Casting down imaginations, and every high thing that [exalts] itself against the knowledge of God, and bringing into captivity every thought to the obedience of Christ" (KJV). Your thoughts are at your command; you can tame them and make them obedient to Christ. Don't let your mind become a workshop for the devil. Instead, keep it occupied with righteousness and peace.

Time to think about it

What is God revealing to me through today's devotion?

_____

_____

_____

_____

What is one specific thing I can do to apply this lesson to my life?

_____

_____

_____

_____

DAY 54:
THE LORD WILL PUT NO MORE ON YOU THAN YOU CAN BEAR

> There hath no temptation taken you but such as is common to man: but God is faithful, who will not suffer you to be tempted above that ye are able; but will with the temptation also make a way to escape, that ye may be able to bear it.
>
> 1 Corinthians 10:13 KJV

As we go through life, we experience seasons of ups and downs, laughter and tears, good times and bad, happy times and sad. Life is mutable. There seems to be this cycle that exists in our lives, and things just naturally follow it. First up, then down, and back up again—life changes. Consider God's servant Job. In the beginning of the book, he is considered the greatest man in the land of Uz. He was called perfect and upright, for he feared God and eschewed evil (see Job 1:1 KJV). Job was on the upside of the wheel of mutability—the father of ten children—seven sons and three daughters, and the owner of a huge home, thousands of sheeps and camels, and hundreds of oxens and asses (Job 1:2-3 KJV). He was wealthy and blessed, and he reverenced God. Then along came Satan who theorized that Job was good only because of his prosperity. "Doth Job fear God for nought?" he asks God. "Has not thou made an hedge about him and about his house, and about all that he hath on every side? Thou has blessed the work of his hands, and his substance is increased in the land. But put forth thine hand now, and touch all that he hath, and he will curse thee to thy face" (Job 1:11 KJV). And so God turned Satan lose on his servant Job, and:

1. The Sabeans attacked first, slaying Job's servants and taking his oxen and asses (Job 1:15 KJV).
2. The fire of God fell from heaven, burning up his sheep and more servants (v. 16 KJV).
3. The Chaldeans then attacked—three bands of them—taking with them the camels and killing even more servants (v. 17 KJV).
4. While Job's children were eating and drinking wine at the oldest brother's house, a great wind came upon them and smote the four corners of the house, causing it to fall upon Job's children, killing them (vs. 18-19 KJV). Note: Here, Job found himself on the downside of the cycle, but he was still able to say, "Naked came I out of my mother's womb, and naked shall I return tither: the LORD gave, and the LORD hath taken away; blessed be the name of the LORD" (v. 21 KJV). Of course, this made the devil unhappy, so he returned to God. "Hmph! Skin for skin, yea, all that a man hath will he give for his life. But put forth thy hand now, and tough his bone and

flesh, and he will curse thee to thy face" (Job 2:4-5 KJV). And God answered, "Behold, he is in thine hand; but save his life" (v. 6 KJV). And so,
5. Job's body was attacked by the enemy and covered with boils (v. 7 KJV).
6. His wife, becoming discouraged, told him to curse God and die. Nevertheless, Job still held fast his integrity (v. 9 KJV).
7. Then along came Job's friends who assumed he had sinned. (After all, the innocent don't suffer; the wicked do.) They directed Job to seek God's forgiveness, reminding him of the blessings he would receive if he repented. They lost confidence in Job and judged him (see vs. 11-13 KJV).

In the midst of Job's troubles, he longed for death, but he would not curse God because he trusted that God would not only vindicate him, but God would eventually reveal to him why all of these things were happening to him. Knowing that he was innocent, Job could only conclude that God destroys the blameless along with the wicked, and in Job 13:5, he said, "Though he slay me, yet will I trust him" (KJV) because Job knew that God would put no more on him than he was able to bear.

Likewise, we must trust God in times of trouble—personal and family troubles and worldwide catastrophes. We must trust him to keep us, to deliver us as he has done for others: the three Hebrew boys in the fiery furnace, Daniel in the lion's den, Joseph in Potiphar's house, Jonah in the belly of the fish, Abraham and Isaac on Mount Moriah, the children of Israel in Egypt, Paul on the road to Damascus, Paul and Silas in an inner prison, and Job in the midst of all his trials.

When we truly realize that God wouldn't bring us to the test if he wasn't able to bring us through it, we will say as the prophet Habakkuk, "Although the fig tree shall not blossom, neither shall fruit be in the vines; the labour of the olive shall fail; and the fields shall yield no meat; the flock shall be cut off from the fold, and there shall be no herd in the stalls; yet I will rejoice in the Lord, I will joy in the God of my salvation" (Habakkuk 3:17–18 kjv).

Time to think about it

What is God revealing to me through today's devotion?

_____

_____

_____

_____

What is one specific thing I can do to apply this lesson to my life?

_____

_____

_____

_____

DAY 55: NOTHING BEATS A FAILURE BUT A TRY

> We are troubled on every side, yet not distressed: we are perplexed, but not in despair; Persecuted, but not forsaken; cast down, but not destroyed.
>
> 2 Corinthians 4:8–9 KJV

Many times, as Christians, we find ourselves being knocked down, kicked around, picked on, lied on, and facing trouble on every side. The Scriptures reassures us that we are in his care, and because of that, we must never give up. Proverbs 24:16 says, "For a just man falleth seven times, and riseth up again." Yes, we get cast down sometimes, not into sin but in our state of mind, in our faith, and perhaps in our image before men. Yet God won't allow us to be destroyed.

We, as the body of Christ, represent a holy God. And we draw a picture of what we believe when we go about our day-to-day lives before men. In drawing a Christ-like picture with our lives, we must distinguish ourselves from the world, showing that Christ has made a difference in our hearts.

First Corinthians 6:20 says, "For ye are bought with a price: therefore glorify God in your body, and in your spirit, which are God's" (KJV). The lives we live and the things that happen to us along the way should be spiritual travels by which we glorify God.

When something knocks us off of our feet, when we get up, we are saying to the world that Christ is greater than anything we may face. The only way we lose is if we don't try. Nothing wins quite like trying again. We must defeat failure with persistent effort for our sufficiency is of God. Second Corinthians 3:2–5 states,

> Ye are our epistles written in our hearts, known and read of all men: forasmuch as ye are manifestly declared to be the epistle of Christ ministered by us, written not with ink, but with the Spirit of the living God; not in tables of stone, but in fleshly tables of the heart. And such trust have we through Christ to God-ward: not that we are sufficient of ourselves to think any thing as of ourselves; but our sufficiency is of God (KJV).

Keep trying. Keep getting up. Doing so testifies the goodness of the God you serve. To stay down makes a mockery of his wonderful grace and power. We have all the motivation and encouragement we need for the psalmist declares, "I have been young, and now am old; yet have I not seen the righteous forsaken nor his seed begging bread" (Psalm 37:25 KJV). God will not allow you to be ashamed, but he will send down the latter rain, having only moderately blessed you with the former (see Joel 2:23 KJV). Get up and beat failure with a try, a trying of the Master.

Time to think about it

What is God revealing to me through today's devotion?

_____

_____

_____

_____

What is one specific thing I can do to apply this lesson to my life?

_____

_____

_____

_____

DAY 56: UNITED WE STAND; DIVIDED WE FALL

> No man can enter into a strong man's house, and spoil his goods, exept he will first bind the strong man; and then he will spoil his house.
>
> Mark 3:27 KJV

Ma Dear loved family. In fact, she loved family to the point of vehemently defending and often upholding some of us in our wrongdoing simply because she loved us and didn't want us to be hurt or to suffer in any way, not even when the sufferings were consequences for our own actions. One thing I will certainly give her credit for is the fact that she united us while she was here on Earth. She believed and trusted the old saying that "United we stand; divided we fall" (John Dickinson, *The Liberty Song*, 1768). Ma Dear was the matriarch of the family, who brought us all together. Her house was our home base. Sadly, since she's been gone, our family has been really struggling to uphold that unyielding bond she created through her love for each of us.

Living with my grandmother taught me that family is one of the most important institutions given to us by God. Family is there for one another, loving and sacrificing, being strength when loved ones are weak and providing shelter from life's storms. I will forever remember our family dinners—not at the dinner table, but sitting in the den with plates in our laps. I will forever remember weeknights in front of the television with Ma Dear watching such a variety of programs to enlighten us of the world around us. From movies to cooking shows to painting shows to the Grammy's to the Olympics—she gathered us to learn.

Ma Dear died in 2004, and my mother's death in 2010 left me the matriarch of our family. I have some very special, amazing shoes to fill. I can only hope that my life unifies as beautifully as hers did. She often told us that we are the only family we have, and if we don't stand together, then we will surely fall. We're such a small family that we seem to be leaning right now, but I know that one day, we will stand tall and Ma Dear's legacy will be that of a family united in love and standing on a rock.

Time to think about it

What is God revealing to me through today's devotion?

_____

_____

_____

_____

What is one specific thing I can do to apply this lesson to my life?

_____

_____

_____

_____

DAY 57: WHY PUT OFF FOR TOMORROW WHAT YOU CAN DO TODAY?

> I must work the works of him that sent me, while it is day; the night cometh, when no man can work.
>
> John 9:4 KJV

If "procrastination is the thief of time" (Edward Young) and there is no time like the present, then why do we put off until tomorrow that which we can do today? I truly admire those who do not put off the inevitable, but it seems to be human nature for some of us to procrastinate. Time management gurus will tell you not to handle a piece of paper twice. When a memo, bill, task, or correspondence comes across your desk, handle it then and be done with it. Yet so many of us will place the document in our Don't Forget folder, before moving it to the To Do folder, before upgrading it to our short list, or before actually move it to the Urgent! Must Do Now pile. We shuffle paper and unnecessarily move it around many times when all we have to do is take care of it the first time we come in contact with the task.

Tomorrow isn't promised to any of us, and the only time we have to fulfill our purpose is here and now. Jesus was our example many times over because he never put off a task that was in his power to perform in the moment. I've never read where he told someone "hold on" or "I'll get back to that later." No, Jesus stopped and healed in the moment that healing was needed. When his miracles were delayed, it wasn't because he procrastinated, but it was so that the power and excellency of God could be magnified in the situation. For example, when Lazarus died, Jesus waited until he returned to Jerusalem before he called Lazarus forth from the grave (see John 11 KJV). Jesus's distance from the city had no bearing on his ability to perform the miracle. He could have called Lazarus from thousands of miles, and Lazarus would have gotten out of his grave. However, in order for man to see and know that it was the power of God at work, Jesus journeyed back, giving the dead body time to begin its decay, before he showed up to save the day.

Our mind should be like Christ Jesus's mind. Let us move when God says move. Let us do what he says do *when* he says do it. The Lord is speaking to many hearts today, calling them to repentance, calling them to ministry, calling them to obedience to him and his Word, and calling them to help their sisters and brothers. And there really is no time like the present to heed his calling. There is no time like the present to be his servant, obedient to him. There is no time like the present to be that blessing to someone else or to walk in the will of God. Today is the day of salvation. Why put it off until tomorrow? The Bible says, "Today, if you hear his voice, harden not your hearts" (Hebrews 3:15 KJV). Do what you can today; hear and obey the voice of God.

Time to think about it

What is God revealing to me through today's devotion?

_____

_____

_____

_____

What is one specific thing I can do to apply this lesson to my life?

_____

_____

_____

_____

DAY 58: WHEN LIFE HANDS YOU LEMONS MAKE LEMONADE

> For we know that all things work together for good to them that love God, to them who are the called according to his purpose.
>
> Romans 8:28 KJV

My grandmother was a rock. She was a woman who took the worst of times and made them into moments of triumph. By the help of God, she could stretch a dollar, improvise, and provide for her family so that they had no idea times were tough. Injured on her job as a nurse's aide and unable to work after surgery on her knees, she supported us with government assistance and determination. She never sat around feeling sorry for herself, but she shook off adversity and rose in victory. We didn't have a lot, but we had love. We had a roof over our heads, heat in winter, and cooling in summer. We had gardens of vegetables; when I think back on some of our meals, it now makes sense to me why we had rice and cornbread with chili beans.

It makes sense to me now why we ate "clean out the refrigerator" soup. It makes sense to me now why some days we had homemade biscuits or pancakes for dinner. It makes sense to me now why some days we ate grits and gravy with bologna or a plate of cabbage greens and cornbread for dinner.

Life handed Ma Dear lemons, and many times, I wondered how she felt about her life overall. It seems that she endured more tests, trials, and adversities than one person should, but she never complained. She never murmured. Instead, she sacrificed her all to care for us and bring a smile to our faces, and she herself lit up when we did. She was faithful to my mother, taking care of her and helping her with us. She took care of her parents when they were sick, caring for them until their deaths. She took in my mother's four children and provided for us when she didn't have to. She worked from the time she married, left home at the age of sixteen, and helped build her home with her own two hands. She struggled and died penniless, saving five thousand dollars the last three years of her life to pay for her own funeral.

Life handed her lemons, but her attitude turned them into lemonade, and I believe she's now sipping on sweet, lemony sunshine, having earned her rest. The Bible says, "But the God of all grace, who hath called us unto his eternal glory by Christ Jesus, after that ye have suffered a while, make you perfect, stablish, strengthen, settle you. To him be glory and dominion for ever and ever" (1 Peter 5:10–11 KJV). Ma Dear, by the grace of God, has become perfect.

Time to think about it

What is God revealing to me through today's devotion?

_____

_____

_____

_____

What is one specific thing I can do to apply this lesson to my life?

_____

_____

_____

_____

DAY 59:
EASY COME; EASY GO!

> And whatsoever ye do in word or deed, do all in the name of the Lord Jesus, giving thanks to God and the Father by him.
>
> Colossians 3:17 KJV

When things are handed to us on a silver platter and we do not have to work for them at all, we tend to appreciate them less than those possessions for which we had to shed some blood, sweat, and tears. When I look back over my life, I find that the things I worked hardest for are the things that brought me the most joy and feeling of accomplishment. The same can be said about the relationships that are a part of our lives. Those relationships that are most worth having are those for which we often have to sacrifice ourselves and work at maintaining. Jesus said, "If any man will come after me, let him deny himself and take up his cross daily, and follow me" (Luke 9:23 KJV). Being a follower of Christ and servant of God is such a privilege and honor. We cannot work for this privilege; it is a gift! Nevertheless, we must recognize that the opportunity to commune with our Heavenly Father did not come easily. It required the life and blood of Jesus Christ to bring us into fellowship with God. No, it didn't come easily for the Lord, and we should not take it for granted when we accept it. I mean to really follow Jesus, we must understand the need to crucify this flesh daily, and we must also be willing to make the sacrifice. We are no longer our own, but we have been purchased by the precious blood of our Lord and Savior, Jesus Christ.

There are other relationships in my life that I have to work at maintaining, and I do it gladly because I cherish the relationship. For example, my marriage requires effort, but as a result of that effort, my husband and I enjoy a beautiful relationship that has been blessed by God. We have to keep the lines of communication open daily and share with one another our thoughts and feelings continually. We must always remember to express our love and affection for one another, and sometimes try to be creative in doing so. We have to regularly humble ourselves and give in to the other person so that peace abides. We don't keep count of our sacrifices for one another but present them willingly that our relationship might continue to grow. Sometimes, we have to give a little more than we take, and that's okay. Any relationship that is worth your participation is going to require total commitment and a decrease in selfish behavior. The fact that marriage is not easy increases the chance that if we stick with it, the results will be lasting.

There are also friendships that I have in my life that really try me, particularly in the area of patience. I accept the challenge of it because I love my friends and want them in my life. Sometimes, I have to say things that the other person doesn't want to hear and vice versa: I have to hear things the other person doesn't necessarily want to say. However, honesty is more important than the regret of not flattering or the discomfort of not pleasing the other person. Those relationships that are hard fought and won are forever.

When things come too easily in life, they can likewise be easily taken. The Bible says, "In all labour there is profit" (Proverbs 14:23 kjv). Working for what we receive leads to profit and an accomplishment that isn't easily taken. When we put in the time and effort and the pain and tears, then joy and laughter follow. An appreciation for the work ensues, and in the end, it is all worth it.

Time to think about it

What is God revealing to me through today's devotion?

_____

_____

_____

_____

What is one specific thing I can do to apply this lesson to my life?

_____

_____

_____

_____

DAY 60: WHAT DOESN'T KILL YOU MAKES YOU STRONGER

> Blessed is the man that endureth temptation: for when he is tried, he shall receive the crown of life, which the Lord hath promised to them that love him.
>
> James 1:12 KJV

One of the most encouraging statements I have ever heard came from a dear friend when I was trying to come up with a topic for a weekly Bible class I teach via conference call. She asked, "Why not this? *God will not protect you from that which he will use to perfect you.*" Initially, I found the statement cumbersome and perhaps wordy. I tried to reword it quickly in my mind, but I kept coming back to the exact way she presented it to me. So I settled on her words, thought about them for a few moments more, uttering them softly, and as the meaning sank in, "Perfect!" I replied. Sometimes, we want God to deliver us from any and every thing that is the least bit uncomfortable, but there are times when the Lord is at work, and he uses the very test we are in the middle of to strengthen us. How encouraging! I believe I can endure just about anything as long as I know the source of the test and the source of my strength are both God Almighty, who only wants what is best for me.

Isaiah 64:8 says, "But now, O Lord, thou art our father; we are the clay, and thou our potter; and we all are the work of thy hand" (KJV). Keep in mind that it is God's desire to bless us, to perfect us, and to use us for his divine purpose. And as we walk through life, there will be times when we feel a need or desire for his protection, an urge to run and hide behind the Master and Creator of us all. There will be times when we want to call 911—that is, Psalm 91:1 that reads, "He that dwelleth in the secret place of the most High shall abide under the shadow of the Almighty" (KJV). We want to seek safety in the shadow of his wing, and there are times when that's what we should do. However, there are times when God is trying to do a new thing in our lives, and he will *not* protect us from that situation or circumstance through which he is trying to perfect us.

The above scripture, Isaiah 64:8, likens us to clay. A lump of shapeless matter scooped from the earth. Yet from our state of emptiness, God fashions vessels that are meet for his use. While we are in the Potter's hands, we undergo many changes—some good, some not so good, some soothing and sweet, and some downright painful and uncomfortable—but they all are the moving and making of the Lord. Stay in his hands, bearing in mind that when we go through the fire, we shall come out as pure gold. In order to experience the perfecting of God, we must go through. Cry out to God, "Don't move my mountain, but give me strength to climb. Don't take away my stumbling blocks, but lead me around [it]" (Mahalia Jackson, *Don't Move My Mountain*).

If we are to be a servant of God, he must call us out of our comfort zone just as he did his servant Moses. When God appeared to Moses with explicit instructions on what he wanted him to do, Moses responded with excuses: they will not believe me, nor hearken unto my voice; they will say that the Lord has not appeared to [me] (Exodus 4:1 KJV); I am not eloquent; I am slow of speech, and of a slow tongue (v. 10 KJV). God didn't accept that. He told Moses, "Who hath made man's mouth? Or who maketh the dumb, or deaf, or the seeing, or the blind? Have not I the LORD? Now therefore go, and I will be with thy mouth, and teach thee what thou shalt say" (v. 11 KJV). God did not protect Moses from the discomfort of his calling, and neither will he accept our excuses to disobey him. It's when we decide "Yes, Lord!" in our spirit that God will go on to perfect us.

If we are to be perfected by God, we must keep our feelings out of our growth and development in the Lord. Sometimes, the Lord allows our feelings to get hurt. Why? Because from that we learn humility, we learn to love, and we learn to forgive. I'm reminded of the Canaanite woman who approached Jesus, crying, "Have mercy on me, O Lord, thou Son of David; my daughter is grievously vexed with a devil" (Matthew 15:22 KJV). Jesus' response to this lady would have had some of us not speaking to the Lord for weeks: "I am not sent but unto the lost sheep of the house of Israel… It is not meet to take the children's bread, and to cast it to dogs" (v. 24 KJV). This woman realized that in order to be perfected, she had to disregard her feelings. Will God protect us from the attitudes, mistreatment, and misunderstanding of others? No, for by these happenings, we learn to humble ourselves as this Canaanite woman. She replied, "Truth, Lord: yet the dogs eat of the crumbs which fall from their masters' tables" (v. 27 KJV). We learn to *really* love with the love of Christ as we obey Jesus's command to "love [our] enemies, bless them that curse [us], do good to them that hate [us], and pray for them which despitefully use and persecute [us]" (Luke 6:27-28 KJV). If the offense doesn't come, we'd never be able to exercise this Word. Finally, we learn to forgive for that is the only way the Heavenly Father will forgive us—when we first forgive one another.

No matter what you're going through, never give up on God. If he brought you to it, he'll bring you through it. "Be of good courage, and he shall strengthen your heart, all ye that hope in the LORD" (Psalm 31:24 KJV).

When the thorn in our side becomes too much to bear, remember what the Lord spoke to the apostle Paul: "My grace is sufficient for thee: for my strength is made perfect in weakness." Like Paul, declare within yourself, "therefore will I rather glory in my infirmities, that the power of Christ may rest upon me" (2 Corinthians 12:9 KJV), knowing that "all things work together for good to them that love God, to them who are the called according to his purpose" (Romans 8:28).

"I have been young, and now am old; yet have I not seen the righteous forsaken, nor his seed begging bread" (Psalm 37:25 KJV). So remember, what doesn't kill you will surely make you stronger (Nietzsche). The Lord will not always protect us from the tests and trials of life, the snares set by the enemy, or the mistreatment by others, for it is through these very things he ultimately wants to perfect us.

Time to think about it

What is God revealing to me through today's devotion?

_____

_____

_____

_____

What is one specific thing I can do to apply this lesson to my life?

_____

_____

_____

_____